Family Health Guide

PREGNANCY

GW00545672

WARD LOCK

FAMILY HEALTH GUIDE

PREGNANCY

JULIA GOODWIN

WITH THE HELP OF THE
HEALTH VISITORS ASSOCIATION

WARD LOCK

Dedication

To Anna, our firstborn; and to Oliver and William, our sons. They are our most precious gifts. To Simon also, my fellow traveller.

"Your children are not your children. For they have their own thoughts. You may house their bodies but not their souls, for their souls dwell in the house of tomorrow, which you cannot visit, not even in your dreams." (Kahlil Gibran).

Author

Julia Goodwin is a writer and journalist who specializes in pregnancy and childcare. She has edited the UK parenting magazines Right Start and Under Five and has written several books. She is married with three children and lives in Sussex, England.

A WARD LOCK BOOK

First published in the UK 1994
by Ward Lock
Villiers House
41/47 Strand
London
WC2N 5JE

A Cassell Imprint

Designed and produced
by SP Creative Design
147 Kings Road, Bury St Edmunds, Suffolk, England
Editor: Heather Thomas
Art Director: Rolando Ugolini
Illustrations: Peter Orrock and A. Milne (pages 39, 47, 57)

Acknowledgements

Cover photograph: Comstock Photo Library
page 16: Bubbles/H.C. Robinson
page 24: Omikron/Science Photo Library
pages 25 & 27: Petit Format/Nestle/Science Photo Library
page 26: Dr M.A. Ansory/Science Photo Library
page 38: James Stevenson/Science Photo Library
page 65: Bubbles/F. Rombout
page 66: Larry Mulvehille/Science Photo Library
page 72 Jim Selby/Science Photo Library

Distributed in the United States
by Sterling Publishing Co., Inc.
387 Park Avenue South, New York, NY 10016-8810

Distributed in Australia
by Capricorn Link(Australia) Pty Ltd
2/13 Carrington Road, Castle Hill, NSW 2154

A British Library Cataloguing in Publication Data
block for this book may be obtained from the British Library.

ISBN 0-7063-7251-4

Printed and bound in Spain

Contents

Introduction   6

Chapter 1   Are you fit to be pregnant?   7

Chapter 2   You and your baby: 0-3 months   13

Chapter 3   You and your baby: 3-6 months   29

Chapter 4   You and your baby: 6-9 months   40

Chapter 5   Getting ready for birth   48

Chapter 6   The birth   56

Chapter 7   Getting to know your baby   70

Chapter 8   Getting back in shape   73

Useful information   79

Index   80

Introduction

"She was lifted high. I remember the length of her body, her perfect legs and feet as she was lowered onto my tummy. And such lovely dark hair! She is so beautiful – I can't believe we made her."

This entry in an old diary, scribbled at night on a maternity ward a day or two after the birth of my eldest child, records my first impression of becoming a parent.

If you have just discovered you are pregnant – or are planning to start a family soon – you may find it hard to imagine the day you will give birth. Perhaps it seems such a long way off that it is impossible to focus your thoughts. You may still be reeling from the shock of discovering you are pregnant – even if the pregnancy was planned – or maybe you feel it is all very unreal and that if you pinch yourself you will wake up.

Your body does not give away many clues about the dramatic changes occurring inside you either. Yet hour by hour, from the moment of conception and throughout the next 40 weeks, it is adapting to the needs of the baby growing inside you – even if at first your shape does not look very different from normal.

The conception and development of a healthy baby may depend partly on how fit and healthy you and your partner are. Even if you have never worried too much about diet and exercise in the past, it is now very important that you take really good care of yourself for the next nine months.

Practical considerations are also very important. How will you cope with the cost of bringing up a child? Should you go back to work? If you do, who will care for the baby? Finding out about maternity benefits and leave and the range of childcare options available will help you to make these important decisions.

And the pregnancy itself may be causing concern. What are the arrangements for ante-natal care? Where should the baby be born and what sort of birth would be best for you both? What happens if there are problems during the pregnancy? Getting familiar with the facts and the choices available to pregnant women about ante-natal care and childbirth will give you the confidence to decide what is right for you.

Ten years after my daughter's birth, and with two sons completing the family picture, parenthood still seems a journey through uncharted territory. The responsibility is awesome; the fun and amusement an unexpected delight. The powerful sense of excitement you now feel at having created a new life should help to sustain you through the difficult times. Good luck on your journey.

Chapter one

Are you fit to be pregnant?

"You feed a house plant if you want it to flower well, you nurture a fruit tree to gain a good crop. By preparing your body for pregnancy you will give your baby the best possible start in life," says Belinda Barnes, Chairman of Foresight, the Association for the Promotion of Pre-Conceptual Care in the UK.

Once you've decided you want to have a baby, getting into good shape before you embark on your pregnancy makes sense. The fitter you are before you get pregnant, the easier it will be for your body to cope with the extra demands of pregnancy and breastfeeding. You will recover more quickly from the birth and cope better with the new responsibilities of parenthood.

Advance planning is important for another reason too. In the twelve weeks after conception all the baby's major organs are formed. Yet no couple can know exactly when they will conceive and it will probably be several weeks afterwards before you are 100 per cent sure that you are pregnant.

During that time your baby's brain, nervous system and heart will be forming. If you have prepared for pregnancy you will know that you have given your baby the best possible chance of being healthy from the moment it was conceived.

In fact, taking care of your health and improving your all-round fitness will actually help you conceive. On average nearly half of British couples having intercourse without contraception take longer than six months to conceive. If you or your partner smokes, drinks heavily or eats a diet lacking in essential nutrients, then your fertility levels may be adversely affected. Just as worrying, you may be more likely to have problems with the pregnancy or even have a baby with a birth abnormality.

So how far in advance should you start to plan for pregnancy and what steps should you be taking to get fit for pregnancy? Most experts recommend that you start preparing for pregnancy three to six months before you hope to conceive. This will give your body time to benefit from a new regime of healthy eating and regular exercise and it will give it time to rid itself of any harmful substances that might affect the healthy development of your baby.

Are you fit to be pregnant?

Drugs and medication

1 If you are on the contraceptive pill this three-month delay is recommended. During that time you should stop taking the Pill and use a barrier method of contraception like the cap or sheath. This will allow time for the level of vitamins and minerals in your blood to return to normal before the onset of pregnancy. Zinc, in particular, is important for maintaining a healthy pregnancy and producing a plentiful supply of milk for breastfeeding. Yet many women have low zinc levels, particularly if they have been on the Pill for some time.

2 You should also tell your doctor that you are planning to conceive if you have been taking other drugs and medications. Diabetes, high blood pressure, acne and asthma are just a few conditions that may be treated with powerful drugs. It may be possible to cut down on the dosage of some long-term medications or to change to alternative ones that will not harm a growing fetus, but you need to sort this out before you try to conceive.

This would also be a good opportunity to discuss your family history, especially if there is evidence of any hereditary conditions, disease or handicap. Your doctor should be able to advise you of the risks of your child being affected.

3 Addictive drugs will affect your fertility and are likely to damage your baby's health. If you are planning to have a baby, you must seek expert help to stop.

Diet

Eating a healthy diet is a vital part of your pre-pregnancy routine. Poor eating habits can lead to problems in conceiving a healthy baby and carrying it to term. You will also feel much fitter and more energetic if you are getting a good balance of essential foods at this special time.

This is also a good time for your partner to review his diet. His sperm can also be affected if he eats unhealthily. Try to change together – after all, it won't be too long before you are planning proper family meals and if you both eat healthily your child will be encouraged to develop healthy eating habits as well.

Healthy eating checklist

1 Increase the amount of raw or lightly cooked fruit and vegetables you eat. Together with starchy carbohydrate foods like bread, pasta, rice and cereals, these should form the main part of any meal.

2 Keep up your protein consumption by eating lean meat, poultry, fish, eggs, cheese, beans and lentils. And remember that

dairy products like milk, cheese and yogurt are important sources of calcium – essential for strong bones and teeth for you and your baby.

3 It is important to take folic acid supplements before you conceive to reduce the risk of having a spina bifida baby. Spina bifida occurs when the baby's neural tube fails to close about three weeks after conception – before many women know they are pregnant.

Now the British Government is advising all women planning to get pregnant to take 0.4 milligrams (400 micrograms) of folic acid each day from the time that they want to conceive until the twelfth week of pregnancy. (Women who have already had a baby with a neural tube defect will be prescribed a much bigger dose by their doctors.) Before you take a supplement, especially if you are on any medication, discuss it with your doctor.

You should also eat plenty of folate-rich foods at this time. A healthy adult needs 0.2mgs of folic acid each day – women who are pregnant or considering pregnancy need a total of 0.6mgs. Foods rich in folic acid include lightly-cooked green vegetables like Brussels sprouts, broccoli, spinach and green beans, as well as whole-grain bread, and rice, yeast extract and orange juice, and fortified foods, e.g. cereals and bread.

4 Liver contains a lot of folic acid but you should avoid eating it if you are planning to conceive and during your pregnancy. This is because liver contains large amounts of vitamin A, which could harm your unborn baby. Avoid foods made from liver, such as faggots, liver pâté and liver sausage. You should also avoid eating any vitamin supplements that contain vitamin A, unless they are prescribed specially by your doctor.

5 Pregnancy is a time when it is important for your blood to have good iron reserves – or a haemoglobin level of 12 or 13. If you have heavy periods you may have low iron stores so, again, you need to build these up in the months before conception. Green leafy vegetables, lean red meat, dried fruit, nuts and sardines all contain iron. Vitamin C is needed to help your body absorb iron from

A healthy, balanced diet will supply all the nutrients you need for your own health and that of your baby. You should establish healthy eating habits now.

Are you fit to be pregnant?

Dental care

Arrange to have a dental check-up as part of your planning for a healthy baby, so that your dentist can carry out treatment before you get pregnant. X-rays and anaesthetic carry some risks for your unborn baby.

Once you are pregnant, the extra progesterone in your body may make your gums swell and bleed and thereby leave your teeth more prone to infection, so it's important to take care of any potential problems beforehand. If you need dental treatment during pregnancy, discuss this with your dentist – he may be able to give you temporary treatment if you wish to wait until after the birth. In the UK, dental treatment is free during pregnancy.

some food, so you should also eat citrus fruit, peppers, tomatoes and green vegetables.

If your iron level is low you may become anaemic during your pregnancy. You will feel tired and breathless, and it will take longer for your body to heal if you have any stitches after the birth, or if you lose a lot of blood at the delivery. Your baby also needs iron and your own stores will get even lower if you breastfeed whilst you are anaemic. You can avoid all these problems by eating lots of iron-rich foods before and during your pregnancy.

Exercise

Exercise is also important. Try to take some form of aerobic exercise three times a week for at least 20 minutes. Brisk walking and swimming are both excellent exercises which you can keep up during your pregnancy.

As well as helping you to lose weight, regular exercise will tone up your muscles, improve your blood circulation, boost your energy levels and increase your stamina. Your body will be better prepared to cope with the extra strain of carrying a baby and you will be less likely to develop any of the less pleasant side-effects of pregnancy, from stretch marks to piles and varicose veins.

Dangers to your unborn baby

1 German measles (rubella)

This is such a mild disease in adults that you may not know that you have it, but it can cause heart, hearing and eyesight problems in children whose mothers have been infected during the first few weeks of their pregnancy. The latest statistics indicate a rise in the number of pregnant women infected with German measles.

If you are not sure whether you have had German measles or if you are immune to the disease ask your doctor for a simple blood test. If necessary, he will then arrange for you to be immunized before you try for a baby.

2 Smoking

Probably the single most important step that you can take for your baby's sake is to give up smoking today – and that applies to your partner, too. Smoking affects the development of healthy sperm. Men who smoke are less fertile than non-smokers and

they are more likely to father damaged babies – the more cigarettes they smoke, the higher the risk.

If you are pregnant and continue to smoke, the carbon monoxide and nicotine will pass straight across the placenta into your developing baby's bloodstream.

The list of dangers to your unborn baby makes chilling reading. If you smoke while you are pregnant you are more likely to miscarry, have a premature or stillborn baby. Your baby is more likely to die from cot death during the first months of life. Also, he has a higher risk of being born with abnormalities such as a hare lip or a cleft palate and is twice as likely to develop a childhood cancer. At school he may do less well than his classmates born to non-smoking parents.

Passive smoking can also affect the health of your unborn baby. Even if you give up smoking, your baby may still be at risk of

Alcohol

Advice on drinking alcohol before and during pregnancy varies. All experts agree, however, that heavy drinking or drinking binges by you or your partner before, as well as during, pregnancy are likely to make conception difficult and increase the chance of having a handicapped baby.

The UK Government recommends

two units of alcohol each week as an acceptable limit once you are pregnant. Foresight, the organization for pre-conceptual care, recommends that both partners should abstain totally from drinking for four months before they try to conceive – this is the length of time it takes for sperm to develop.

Are you fit to be pregnant?

Have a check up

Don't wait for your pregnancy to be confirmed before visiting the doctor – have a check-up now. If you have a medical condition, it can be treated before you conceive. Your doctor will also advise you on good nutrition and getting fit for pregnancy.

being born underweight if you are exposed to tobacco smoke during your pregnancy. And he will be more likely to suffer from severe respiratory illness, such as bronchitis, pneumonia or asthma, if he lives in a household of smokers.

3 Sexually transmitted disease

STDs – also called genito-urinary infections – have increased dramatically over the last few decades. If left untreated, they increase the risk of miscarriage, stillbirth and having a handicapped baby. If you suspect that either you or your partner may have been in contact with an STD, then you need to get it diagnosed and treated without delay.

Go to your doctor, or to a specialist hospital clinic if you prefer to remain anonymous You will find the nearest clinic in your local phone book.

If you are HIV positive there is a one in five chance of the virus being passed on to your baby. The chance of having a non-infected baby increases if you are fit and healthy. Remember that the HIV virus can be passed on by having unprotected sex during pregnancy so use a condom.

4 Work hazards

Hazards at work can also be a threat to your health if you plan to conceive. If you work with chemicals, gases, metals or radiation, you should talk to your employer or union representative and to your doctor. If you are at risk, your employer must offer you an alternative job if there is one available.

If you are still anxious, you can contact Foresight in the UK (see page 79). For a fee, they can arrange for samples of your hair to be analysed to check the levels of toxins present in your body and will advise you on the best course of action.

5 Toxoplasmosis

Toxoplasmosis is a disease that can damage children born to infected mothers. As with rubella, the worry is that you may not even realise you have it. Toxoplasmosis can be caught from cats' faeces, undercooked meat, unwashed fruit and vegetables and from contaminated soil. Wear gloves when gardening and avoid emptying cat litter trays while you are trying to conceive and during your pregnancy.

Summary

Pregnancy is a very special time, one that you want to enjoy and look back on with pleasure. If you and your partner take extra care of yourselves now, you can enjoy the next nine months, confident that you have given your baby a flying start on his journey into the world.

Chapter two

You and your baby: 0 - 3 months

Emotions

"I keep bursting into tears, and it's all so overwhelming. I can't concentrate at work and I just feel as if my life is being taken over. I'm tired and pathetic."

However much you planned to have a baby, having your pregnancy confirmed can

provoke mixed emotions. If the baby is unplanned, even though you have decided to continue with the pregnancy, you may be wrestling with the fear of being trapped. There is a powerful feeling of inevitability about it all – birth and motherhood are coming nearer, day by day, and you have no control over this process.

You might also feel that you have to put on a front. Your relatives and friends are usually delighted at the news and expect you to be equally excited. Some days you do feel this way – but at other times you are tired, confused or want to think about other things.

Health professionals can sometimes unwittingly contribute to this feeling of your life being taken over – they may make you feel like a 'patient' carrying another 'patient'. To them the well-being of the baby seems all-important and they expect you to make some decisions about ante-natal care and childbirth before you are familiar with the facts. However, remember that they are there to help you: to allay your anxieties and give you further information so that you can make an informed choice about the type of care that is right for you.

You and your baby: 0 - 3 months

Hormones

The massive hormonal changes taking place inside your body are usually held responsible for any emotional upsets, as well as for the tiredness and nausea that many women experience in the early months. However, is it really surprising that you are on an emotional see-saw? Pregnancy and motherhood change your life dramatically for ever. There may be no other human experience that is so profound or has such long-lasting consequences. Don't be afraid if it takes time to adjust to the idea of being pregnant. Most women feel like this.

You may be reading this and find that it does not relate to your feelings at all. Some women's joy and excitement at becoming pregnant remains with them during the whole pregnancy, making it one of the happiest and most fulfilling times of their lives.

Body changes in early pregnancy

The earliest sign of pregnancy is a missed period. Other signs include:

● **Feeling tired** The dramatic changes that are occurring in your body account for the lethargy and exhaustion that many pregnant women feel. Your energy levels should build up again at about twelve weeks.

Your uterus and heart

Your uterus grows dramatically during pregnancy. Before you become pregnant it is about the size of a satsuma – 7.5cm/ 3 inches long, 5cm/2 inches wide and 2.5cm/1 inch thick. By six weeks it is the size of an apple; at eight weeks it is the size of an average orange. By ten weeks it is as big as a large orange, and by twelve weeks it is as large as a grapefruit. Your heart starts working harder from week 10, when the blood supply to your uterus, breasts and other organs starts to increase.

● **Needing to empty your bladder more often** Hormonal changes relax your muscles, and your growing uterus pushes against the bladder. However, this sensation will ease off at about twelve weeks when the uterus expands out of the pelvis.

● **Changes in your breasts** They may feel tender and tingly. You will notice that the veins appear blue and more prominent under your skin, and the area around your nipples – the areola – gets darker with small nodules standing out.

● **Feeling nauseous** About half of pregnant women suffer from 'morning sickness', although this can occur at any time of day and is often worst in the evening.

● **Being constipated** Eat high-fibre foods, fresh fruit and vegetables and make sure you drink plenty of fluid to counteract this tendency, which is caused by the hormones relaxing your bowel.

Avoid morning sickness by:

1 Getting up slowly in the morning.

2 Eating a dry biscuit and having a drink before you get out of bed.

3 Avoiding fatty foods and cooking smells that make you feel nauseous.

4 Having a bowl of cereal and milk before you go to sleep.

5 Eating little and often – keep a packet of dry biscuits handy. This raises your blood sugar level. Try half a baked potato or sipping soda water to settle your stomach.

6 Wearing loose clothes around your stomach.

7 Avoiding strong-smelling soaps and perfumes.

• **A strong metallic taste in the mouth** You may go off certain foods e.g. coffee, alcohol and fried foods, and develop strange cravings. Your sense of smell is more acute.

• **A thickening waistline** Although some women notice little change before the twelfth week of pregnancy, others find that they cannot do up zips and buttons much earlier than this. Don't worry if this happens to you; it is perfectly normal and definitely not a sign to cut back on your food intake, provided that you are eating a balanced and healthy diet.

Ante-natal care

You may have already carried out your own pregnancy test or have visited your doctor or family planning clinic to have your pregnancy confirmed. You must consult your doctor as soon as possible so that he can arrange your ante-natal care.

You will have regular monthly check-ups either with your doctor, midwife or at the local hospital ante-natal clinic, and as your pregnancy progresses the check-ups will become more frequent.

The first and most detailed one usually occurs between the eighth and twelfth weeks of pregnancy. You will be asked a lot of

Be prepared

Write down any questions you have before you go for your ante-natal check, as it is easy to feel overwhelmed and forget what you planned to ask. Medical staff are pleased to provide information if they know what you want to know!

questions about your family's medical history, and your weight, height and blood pressure will be recorded. You will also have to give samples of blood and urine for testing.

Usual screening procedures include:

1 **Urine test** This checks for sugar, protein and ketones – if these substances are present in your urine you may be suffering from diabetes or pre-eclampsia (a serious illness which may affect some pregnant women). If so you must seek medical help immediately.

2 **Weighing you** This measures the baby's growth and checks for pre-eclampsia.

3 **Taking your blood pressure** This is another pre-eclampsia check.

4 **Examining you for swelling** This is to check for pre-eclampsia.

5 **Feeling your uterus through your abdomen** This checks on the growth and position of the baby.

6 **Listening to the baby's heartbeat** This is to check that it is normal (it is not possible to hear this until about 14 weeks).

7 **Blood tests** These are to check your blood group and Rhesus factor (if it is the more rare Rh–factor, you may need anti-d following delivery); your haemoglobin level (if this is low you may be prescribed a course of iron tablets); to check your immunity to rubella (German measles); and to check for sexually transmitted diseases and hepatitis B.

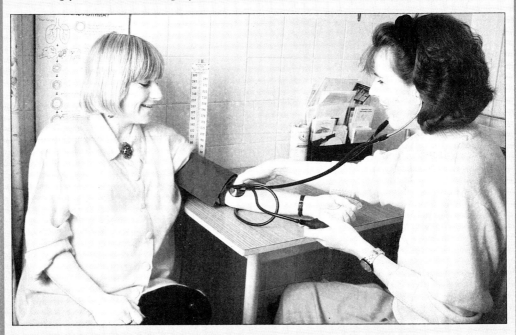

Special testing

Some tests are carried out on different groups of women, depending on their age, medical history and ethnicity. These include:
1 Blood test – to check for sickle cell anaemia, a genetic and disabling disease affecting some Afro-Caribbean babies.
2 Blood test – for thalassaemia, a rare blood disease which may affect some women from India, south-east Asia and the Mediterranean.
3 Blood test – for Tay Sachs disease, a severe disabling disease affecting some Jewish women.
4 Blood test – to check for toxoplasmosis. You usually have to request this.
5 Blood test – to check for HIV (some hospitals take part in an anonymous sampling programme in the UK).

Weight gain

You must expect to put on between 20 and 30lbs during your pregnancy (9-13.5 kg); some women put on more. If you were underweight before you became pregnant you may benefit from a bigger weight gain. You should not *try* to remain slim as eating a low-calorie diet may not provide the essential nutrients that both you and your baby need during this important time. If you eat a healthy, balanced diet which is low in fat and high in protein, vitamins, minerals and carbohydrates, you should not gain excessive weight. If you are seriously overweight before you get pregnant your doctor may recommend a calorie-controlled diet. However, you *must not* diet without informing your doctor and midwife first.

Your weight gain is made up as follows:

Weight of baby –	38%
Weight of placenta –	9%
Weight of amniotic fluid –	11%
Weight of uterus and breasts –	20%
Weight of extra blood –	22%

Diet

Follow the advice given in Chapter One on healthy eating. Your diet is very important during pregnancy. In fact, your baby depends on it too, as does the developing placenta. By trying to eat a balanced diet, you can help reduce the risk of having a premature or difficult labour.

However, do not feel that you have to eat foods you loathe just because you are told that they are 'good' for you.

Vegetarian diets

If you are vegetarian and do not eat animal products, you are relying on vegetable products, which do not contain the same number of amino acids as animal protein. This means that it is difficult for your body to use the proteins for body building. Try to combine beans with a wheat product at the same meal (e.g. lentils with whole-wheat bread, chickpeas with pasta) to enable your body to use the proteins efficiently.

General healthy eating tips during pregnancy

1 Pregnant women need about 75g/3oz protein each day (twice as much as non-pregnant women). Try to have three helpings a day, one from each of the following categories:
- Meat, fish, 2 eggs, cup of nuts
- 120g/4oz hard cheese, 240g/8oz cottage cheese, 550ml/1 pint milk (you can use soya, nut milk or tofu)
- 4 slices whole-grain bread, a helping of brown rice, a helping of whole-grain pasta, a large jacket potato

2 Eat a salad every day. Use chopped cabbage or grated carrot rather than lettuce to add variation to your diet.

3 Make sure you are getting enough vitamins and minerals in your food. Do not rely on supplements alone.

4 Cut down on fatty foods – your body needs very little of them. Boil, steam, grill or oven-bake foods rather than frying them. Try cutting down on chocolate, biscuits and cakes, and eat them only in moderation.

5 Cut down on sugar and sugary drinks – your body does not need them. Sugar contains no nutrients – only empty calories.

6 Make sure that eggs are always cooked thoroughly – the whites and yolks should be solid, to avoid the risk of salmonella food poisoning.

7 Avoid pâtés and soft cheeses like brie and camembert because of the risk of listeria, which can harm your unborn baby.

8 Don't eat liver or liver products.

9 Drink only pasteurized or UHT milk.

10 Drink five or six glasses of water each day to help your kidneys to excrete waste products efficiently.

11 Eat plenty of fruit and vegetables.

Vitamins and minerals

Vitamin A Avoid supplements as too much of this vitamin could harm your baby. It is found in green and orange vegetables, liver and dairy foods, and helps your body to resist infection.

Vitamin B This is divided into four categories – B1 (thiamine), B2 (riboflavin), B6 (pyridozine) and B12 (cyano-cobalamin). It is an important vitamin, helping tissue growth and enabling your body to make use of proteins and carbohydrates. Whole grains, yeast and meat are all important sources of vitamin B. Vitamin B12 helps to form the baby's central nervous system and your haemoglobin; it is present in meat and fish.

Pantothenic acid Pregnant women need nearly double the normal amount of this vitamin, which is present in most foods, especially meat, cheese, eggs, whole-grain cereals and peanuts. It maintains the red blood cells and is essential for the body to break down fat and carbohydrate.

Folic acid This helps the baby's nervous system to develop properly. See page 9 for more details.

Vitamin C This is found in citrus fruit (oranges, lemons and grapefruit), broccoli, blackcurrants and potatoes. It helps to form bones and connective tissue, maintains blood vessels and assists the body to absorb iron.

Vitamin D This helps to form and maintain bones by assisting with the absorption of calcium. It is found in butter, egg yolk, milk, oily fish and sunlight.

Vitamin E Most foods, especially wheatgerm, and vegetable oils, contain vitamin E, which keeps the blood cells healthy.

Vitamin K This is present in all green, leafy vegetables. It makes the blood clot.

Iron This is essential to help your body form red blood cells which carry oxygen to your baby. You need twice as much iron as non-pregnant women. If you do not get sufficient iron, you will feel very tired and may suffer from anaemia. Green, leafy vegetables, red meat, dried fruit and nuts are all very good sources. Vitamin C will help your body to absorb the iron you take in in your food.

Calcium This is necessary for the formation of strong bones and healthy teeth. Your baby's teeth start to bud early in pregnancy so your calcium intake is important. Calcium is found in milk, cheese, yogurt, sardines, whitebait and green vegetables.

Zinc A deficiency of zinc may result in miscarriage or stillbirth. Zinc may also help the muscles to contract during labour. It is present in high-fibre foods, especially bran, nuts and hard cheese. However, taking an iron supplement can interfere with the zinc levels in the body.

You and your baby: 0 - 3 months

Exercise and rest

If you attend a regular exercise class or sports club, let your teacher or coach know that you are pregnant. Many sports centres and health clubs now run special exercise classes, swimming and yoga sessions for pregnant women. Phone your local sports centre or ask your midwife for details.

　　If you are used to strenuous activity like running, you may prefer to change to a gentler form of exercise. Squash and horse riding should be avoided. During the early months of pregnancy your blood pressure drops and this can make you feel dizzy and faint if you run or stand for any length of time. Talk to your doctor about this and see what he recommends. It is important to continue some form of exercise throughout your pregnancy. Although you are putting

Walking is a good way of building exercise into your everyday routine. Relaxing and enjoyable, it helps to keep you fit and builds endurance and strong muscles.

Dental care

If you have not already done so, you must pay a visit to your dentist. Your body is producing higher levels of progesterone, which softens your gums and makes them liable to bleeding and infection. Do tell your dentist that you are pregnant – he needs to know this in case an X-ray is necessary or if antibiotics may be prescribed for an infection. These can be potentially harmful to a growing baby in the womb.

　　You should also pay extra attention to cleaning your teeth. Look after them well during pregnancy and floss between them to get rid of plaque and bacteria.

on weight and your shape is changing, you do not need to develop sagging abdominal muscles. A regular exercise routine will strengthen your muscles and joints, improve your circulation and ease backache. This will help your body to cope with its heavier load. As well as toning your muscles, exercise is also an excellent form of relaxation, and it maintains your body's fitness for the strenuous activity of giving birth. The first few weeks of looking after a new baby are very tiring; if your body is in good condition your energy levels will be higher and you will be better able to cope.

What sort of birth?

You may be asked to make a decision about the type of birth you want on your first visit to the ante-natal clinic. If you have not yet made up your mind do not be afraid to ask for more time to make an informed choice.

Talk to your doctor, midwife and the local supervisor of midwives at your nearest maternity hospital about the choices available. If you are considering a hospital birth you need to find out about policies on inducing and monitoring the baby, episiotomies and moving around during labour. Is there a special care baby unit at the hospital? Ask friends who have recently given birth about their experiences. Go and have a look at your local hospital facilities. Then discuss the issue carefully with your partner. It is very important that you get the right birth for you. In the UK, you have four main options as detailed here:

1 In the consultant unit at the local maternity hospital. You will be under the supervision of a consultant obstetrician and will have some ante-natal checks at the hospital and others in your doctor's surgery if a shared care system operates. You will be delivered by hospital midwives or hospital doctors if there are complications.

2 In a GP unit in hospital in the UK. Your ante-natal care takes place in the local clinic and at home and is given by your family doctor and community midwives, who will also deliver you. The birth takes place in hospital with back-up services available if there are any complications. Many women feel this system combines the security of a hospital environment with the personal and continuous care offered by local midwives.

3 The Domino scheme. This operates in the UK. The local community midwives are responsible for your ante-natal care, often sharing it with your family doctor. The delivery takes place in hospital by the community midwife and you are able to leave hospital as soon as six hours after the birth. This option is not available in every area.

4 At home. Only four per cent of births in the UK take place at home and doctors are often cautious about a home birth for a first

Action plan – the first three months

These first three months of pregnancy have been fairly dramatic. For the first six weeks you may not have even realised that you were pregnant! Now you are faced with lots of important decisions, even although you may still be adjusting to the very idea of being pregnant.

Use the checklist below to make sure that you have done everything necessary to make your pregnancy a positive and rewarding experience.

1 Visit your doctor as soon as you suspect that you are pregnant.

2 Make sure you attend your first ante-natal appointment. You may wish to take along a list of written questions.

3 Find out as much as you can about childbirth options available.

4 Find out about sport and exercise classes for pregnant women in your area.

5 Adopt a healthy balanced diet.

6 Stop smoking and persuade your partner to stop smoking too.

7 Visit your dentist for a check up.

8 Get plenty of rest and relaxation.

baby. However, the community midwives are legally bound to deliver you at home if that is your choice. Your ante-natal care takes place at home and in the local clinic, usually shared with your family doctor. Think about how long it would take the obstetric flying squad to reach you if there was an emergency and what sort of support you would have at home afterwards. There is a move towards making home birth an easier option for women, and, as statistics show, it can be very safe, provided that it is properly planned. **Note:** In addition to these options you can choose to give birth in a private hospital or privately at home, with an independent midwife in attendance.

Your baby's development: 0-3 months

Between twelve and sixteen days before the expected start of your next period you release an egg from your ovary. Every girl baby is born with about half a million potential eggs, and once menstruation begins between 100 and 150 of these eggs start to ripen each month. Normally just one reaches full maturity so it can be fertilized by a male sperm.

Only one in ten of the 400 million sperm present in an ejaculation reaches the cervical canal; the rest are destroyed by acidity in the vagina. It is thought this is one way in which nature cuts down the chance of malformed or weak sperm fertilizing the female egg, as only the strong and healthy sperm are capable of swimming fast enough to survive.

Fertilization

One sperm is 'helped' by many others to penetrate the egg (ovum) and fertilize it. Despite all the advances of modern science, no one is sure exactly how this occurs. It is thought that lots of sperm swim hard into the ovum, causing a chemical reaction that forces the impenetrable gel-like substance surrounding the egg to change to liquid. One sperm then swims through the liquid and manages finally to fertilize the egg, leaving its lashing tail outside. Fertilization can occur as quickly as just one hour after intercourse taking place.

During the next few hours the sperm and egg fuse, forming a single nucleus. The 'blueprint' for a new human being has already been made and all its physical characteristics are already determined. The cell then divides into two and these cells divide and so on for the next 266 days, by which time the baby is fully formed and ready to be born.

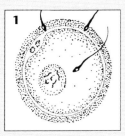 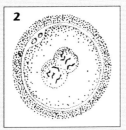 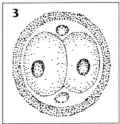 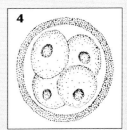

1 A sperm penetrates the ripened egg, which has been released by one of the ovaries. 2 The head of the sperm, the gene-carrying nucleus, separates from the tail and fuses with the egg's nucleus. 3 The egg divides into two cells as the chromosomes of the two nuclei pair off. 4 Cell division continues as the egg makes its journey along the fallopian tube towards the uterus. Right: the female reproductive organs showing the progression of the egg along the fallopian tube. About a week after fertilization the egg embeds itself in the uterine lining.

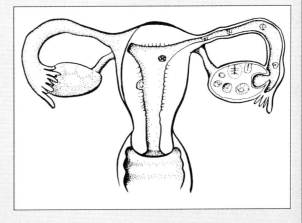

23

You and your baby: 0 - 3 months

Weeks 3 - 4

Seven days after leaving the ovary the fertilized egg completes its journey along the fallopian tube and arrives at the uterus. By this time it is a clustered ball of cells, rather like a blackberry with a hollow centre. On the tenth day the 'blastocyst', as it is called, embeds itself in the lining of the womb. It is now three weeks since your last period and you are classified as being three weeks' pregnant, even though you have not yet missed your next period. The cluster of cells, now just visible to the naked eye, starts to develop into the baby, the amniotic sac and the placenta.

Week 5

This is a crucial time as the baby's nervous system starts to develop. The neural tube is formed by the top layer of cells folding up and round. This develops into the brain and spinal cord. The heart is also forming and the baby has some of its own blood vessels. A string of these vessels will form the umbilical cord connecting the baby to the placenta. Your period is now one week overdue and you may suspect that you are pregnant and start to feel the early signs.

Week 6 - 7

The embryo is now the size of a kidney bean. It develops from the head down, so the lower part of its back looks like a tail. The back of the embryo develops faster than the front, and it grows in an inward curve and looks rather like a sea horse. It has a head, neck, brain and heart and tiny buds which will eventually become arms and legs.

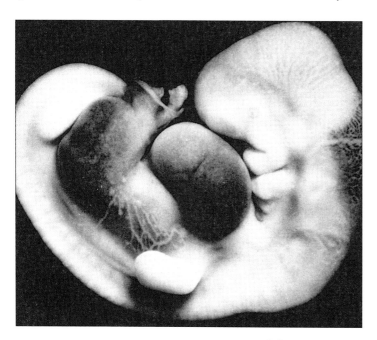

This fascinating photograph, taken from outside of the womb, shows the embryo after 31 days development. Already its heart , brain and blood vessels are developing, although it looks a little like a sea horse.

Embryonic development

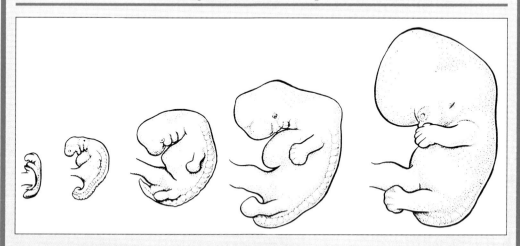

The sequence of illustrations above shows the development of the embryo as it grows rapidly and becomes a recognisable human being. By the end of the second month, it has a head, trunk, tiny limbs, nostrils, lips, tongue, and little webbed fingers and toes. It has the beginnings of a circulatory system and all its major internal organs are developing. Its head is still enormous in relation to its tiny body.

Left: this photograph shows the embryo five to six weeks after fertilization, floating in the amniotic sac, which is filled with fluid protecting the embryo from external pressure. At this stage the embryo is about 15mm long and the umbilical cord is formed. The liver, heart, stomach and sex organs have also begun to develop.

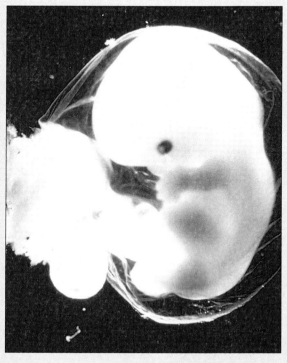

You and your baby: 0 - 3 months

Weeks 7 - 10

From the ninth week, the baby starts to be called a fetus, rather than an embryo. The inner part of the ear is completely formed and the external part is beginning to grow. The bumps at the back of the head and neck are disappearing. The fetus is 4.5cm/1¾ inches long. It looks more and more like a human baby, although the head is still large when compared to the size of the body.

Week 11

The baby is as long as your little finger (5.5cm/2¼ inches). It is easily recognisable as a small human baby, although its limbs are small and thin because the muscles have not yet developed. The internal sex organs – ovaries or testicles – have developed and the external genitals are forming but it is not yet possible to tell the baby's sex. Its heart is pumping blood to all parts of the body.

Week 12

The baby is now 6.5cm/2½ inches long and it weighs 18gm. Its eyelids have developed, and its brain and muscles are co-ordinating to enable it to practise its breathing. It is also kicking, curling its toes, clenching its fists, pressing its lips together and even making some facial expressions.

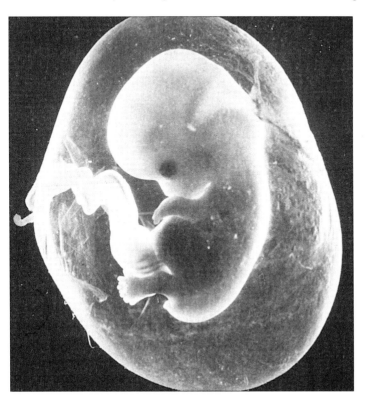

At eight weeks, the fetus floats in the fluid-filled amniotic sac, which is bound by two membranes: the inner amnion and outer chorion. You can clearly see the umbilical cord which forms the link between the fetal and maternal circulations. The end of the eighth week marks the point at which the embryo becomes a fetus.

All the essential organs are now formed and most are beginning to function. For the rest of the pregnancy the baby grows and matures. The major risk period for drugs and infections is over – the baby's development is unlikely to be disturbed by them from now on, although substances such as alcohol and tobacco will still cross the placenta into the baby's bloodstream.

By the twelfth week of pregnancy the baby is beginning to exert pressure on the walls of the uterus, making it grow bigger.

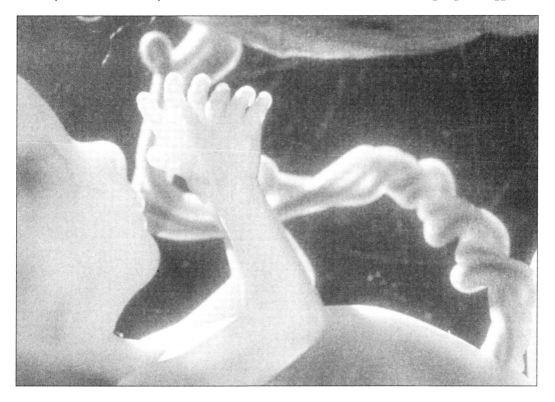

In this picture of the fetus in its fourth month of development, the umbilical cord is visible. This connects the fetus to the placenta: its own life support system and the lifeline between you and your baby. It transports oxygen and nourishment to the fetus and carries away wastes. At no time does your blood flow directly into the fetus; it can only pass through the tissues on your side of the placenta into the baby on the other side. A membrane separates your bloodstream from that of the fetus and the two never mingle. The placenta is fully developed by the twelfth week, and it acts as a filter. Everything you eat, drink or even inhale can pass through the placenta to the fetus so it is important to eat a healthy diet and lead a sensible lifestyle along the lines already discussed.

The placenta

The baby is now starting to rely on the placenta, which develops from the chorionic villi, or finger-like protrusions, which grew around the embryo and provided early nourishment. The villi around the spot where the cluster of cells first embedded itself in the uterus grow rapidly, developing into the placenta, whilst the remaining villi surrounding the embryo die off.

The placenta provides oxygen and nourishment for the baby and removes any waste products. It also passes your antibodies across to the baby and filters out some harmful substances. It produces the right levels of oestrogen and progesterone: two hormones that are essential for sustaining your pregnancy.

It takes 30 seconds for blood to flow from the baby's heart to the placenta and back again via the umbilical cord. By the fourth month of pregnancy 27.5 litres/60 pints of blood will be passing through the placenta each day.

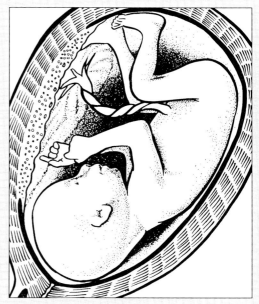

Above: Blood circulates through the umbilical cord and deoxygenated blood is pumped out by the heart back to the placenta together with waste products for excretion. Eating a nutritious diet will help the placenta to grow large and healthy.

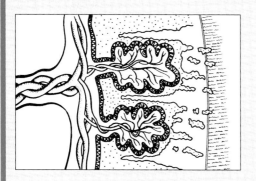

Left: this cross-section through the placenta shows the maternal arteries and veins and the umbilical cord. Your blood filters through the intervillous spaces. Nutrients can also slip through and be transferred to the fetus. However, do remember that potentially harmful substances can also percolate through this sieve, including cigarette smoke, alcohol, drugs and toxic chemicals. Try to avoid these during your pregnancy.

Chapter three

You and your baby: 3 - 6 months

Emotions

"I heard the heartbeat – very fast and quite faint. So now I know I'm definitely pregnant and that it's not all a dreadful mistake." During the middle three months of their pregnancy many women experience a surge of energy and a feeling of well-being. Your tiredness and nausea should decrease and your growing body shows the world that you are carrying a new life within you.

During this third of your pregnancy (called a 'trimester') you will hear the baby's heart beat through the doctor's sonic aid (this is usually around weeks 12-14) and you will also feel the baby moving inside you (you should feel this first between weeks 18-20). At last the pregnancy feels real and you can start to build up a picture of your unborn child. Scans and other tests provide detailed information about the baby, which starts to

develop a personality. Its heart beats fast – or slowly. You feel the baby's movements inside you at a regular time each day. That is when you know it is awake and active.

Gradually the birth starts to feel closer, but the relentless passing of the weeks can bring anxiety. Will the birth be painful? How will you cope? What if you 'fail' in some way or lose control?

Other worries about the baby's well-being and your own adequacy as a mother may also surface. Nobody has taught you how to bring up a child; what if you find the task too difficult? You may wonder whether your baby is fit and healthy and if it will be born without any illness or handicap. Vivid, frightening dreams about giving birth are common; talk about them to your partner, your doctor and your ante-natal teacher.

Body changes

Your body continues to adapt to the needs of the baby growing inside you in the following ways:
1 **Uterus** By week 17 the top of your uterus reaches halfway between your pubic bone

and your navel. By week 20 it is level with your navel and by week 24 it has risen above it. At the beginning of your pregnancy the uterus softens, making it difficult to feel. However, after week 12, when it rises out of

Good posture

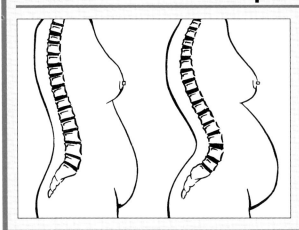

Good posture is vital for avoiding backache when you are pregnant. The better your posture, the stronger your spine and abdominal muscles and the more comfortable you will feel. Try to walk, sit and stand with your back straight as shown (left). Do not thrust your stomach out further, exaggerating the curve of your spine (right). Drop your shoulders to keep your spine straight and ease out tension. Lift your ribs and chest so that you have sufficient space to breathe well.

the pelvis, the top of the uterus can be felt as a hard ridge of muscle.

2 Heart Your heart continues to work harder as the blood supply increases to supply the breasts, uterus, kidneys and other organs. Halfway through pregnancy the uterus requires about 25 per cent of the total blood supply, which increases by as much as 40 per cent. To cope with the increased demand, the heart enlarges and increases its rate by 10 beats per minute, from 70 to 80 beats. This means that it has to beat an extra

Blood supply

Note: The rapid increase in blood supply means that your body must also make more red blood cells; otherwise you will become anaemic.

14,000 times each day! As your pregnancy progresses, the heart is pushed further up into the chest.

3 Pelvis You may suffer from backache as your growing uterus tips your pelvis forward. The ligaments supporting the pelvis soften to enable the bones to widen during pregnancy and labour. Try to stand upright, tucking your pelvis beneath you, and wear shoes that support your feet to prevent your back and foot ligaments from being overstretched.

4 Lungs Although your lungs do not change in shape or size during pregnancy, they have to adapt to working in an increasingly small space inside your chest. This is because the uterus pushes on the ribcage. As your pregnancy progresses you may notice that you take occasional deep or sighing breaths; don't worry – this is quite normal.

Tests to detect abnormalities

In addition to the regular ante-natal tests you undergo at each monthly appointment there are a series of special screening procedures that usually take place during this stage of your pregnancy. By now the pregnancy is firmly established and the growing baby is sufficiently well-developed for tests and scans to be effective. The tests include:

1 Ultrasound scan This is sometimes used several times during a pregnancy for different purposes. The first scan, which usually takes place at about 16 weeks, measures the baby's growth. It is accurate enough to confirm the delivery date within 10 days.

A scan can also be used to detect twins, to pick up handicaps and heart disease and, later on in pregnancy, it shows the exact position in which the baby is lying. It can also monitor the health of the placenta.

It is carried out with a transducer, which picks up echoes of sound waves bounced off your baby as it passes over your tummy. These are recorded as a picture on a screen. The picture may look very blurred, even late on in pregnancy, so do ask the operator to interpret it for you.

Although ultrasound scans are without doubt much safer than X-rays, there has been speculation that the high frequency

Ultrasound scans

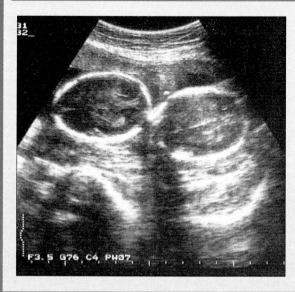

An ultrasound scan is a marvellous opportunity to actually see the baby inside you. To the untrained eye, the scan may appear blurred, so ask the operator to explain the picture on the screen to you. This will help you to distinguish the sometimes confusing shapes and images. If you are lucky, you may see your baby kicking its legs or sucking its thumb. This ultrasound scan picture shows that the mother is expecting twins.

You and your baby: 3 - 6 months

sounds might affect the unborn baby's hearing in some way. The long-term effects of scanning are still being researched, and you should discuss any anxieties you may have with your doctor.

2 Alpha-feto-protein (AFP) testing AFP is produced naturally by the baby. Abnormally high levels present in the mother's blood may indicate that the baby may be suffering from a neural tube defect such as spina bifida or anencephaly.

The level rises later on in pregnancy as a matter of course, so this simple blood test is usually carried out before the eighteenth week. A high level can also mean that you are expecting twins or that the pregnancy is more advanced than originally thought. A scan will then be used to check these possibilities and an amniocentesis test may be offered to you.

3 Amniocentesis Under local anaesthetic, a hollow needle is inserted into the uterus to remove a sample of the amniotic fluid in which the baby is lying. The fluid has been swallowed by the baby and contains cells from the baby's skin. This test is usually

carried out between 16 and 18 weeks.

The test can detect spina bifida, Down's syndrome and other genetic birth defects. In the UK, amniocentesis is offered to every woman over 35 years of age, as the risk of producing a Down's syndrome baby increases sharply at this age, and to women with a strong family history of Down's syndrome.

The technique carries a one per cent risk of miscarriage and you may have to wait several weeks for the result. This could mean having a late termination. It is advisable to accept counselling before the test so that if any difficult decisions have to be made, you and your family can be supported through it.

4 Blood screening The 'Triple' or 'Triple Plus' test is carried out at 15-22 weeks. It assesses the risk factor for spina bifida, anencephaly and Down's syndrome. The 'Triple' test combines the AFP test with two others and is regarded as a more reliable indicator of the need for an amniocentesis. A blood sample, taken by your doctor or midwife, is sent off for testing. There is usually a charge for this, as the test is still undergoing trials in the UK.

Ante-natal classes

Most classes do not begin until the final three months of pregnancy but you need to book in well before this to guarantee a place. In the UK ante-natal classes are offered free by the National Health Service, run by your hospital or community midwife. In addition,

the National Childbirth Trust offers classes nationwide through its local branches. These classes are small, they are often held in the evenings and many include fathers. For attending a course of eight classes, there is a fee. Other private practitioners, including

Ante-natal exercises: Tummy strengthener

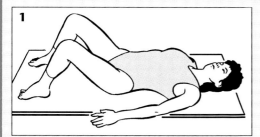

1 Lie on the floor with knees bent and slightly apart. 2 Lift your head and shoulders slightly off the floor and reach out with your right hand to touch your left knee. 3 Lower your head and shoulders gently to the floor and repeat to the other side. Start off with 5 repetitions each side.

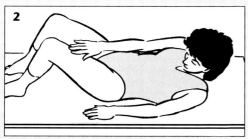

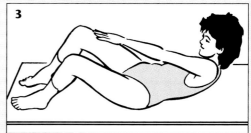

Ante-natal exercise: Abdominal toner

Lie with knees bent, feet hip distance apart. Cross your arms, exhale and raise your head and shoulders and roll up slowly. Hold for a count of 5, pulling in your abdominal muscles and pressing down with your hands. Inhale and lower head and shoulders. Repeat 5 times.

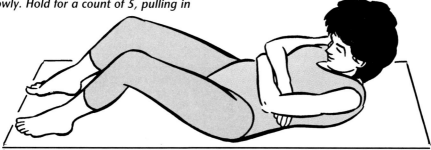

Ante-natal exercises: Pelvic tilting

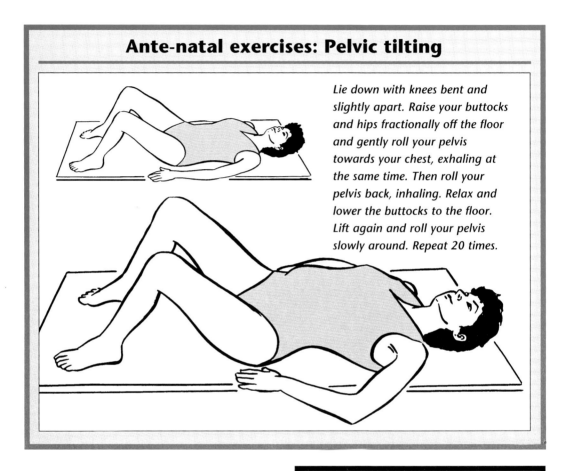

Lie down with knees bent and slightly apart. Raise your buttocks and hips fractionally off the floor and gently roll your pelvis towards your chest, exhaling at the same time. Then roll your pelvis back, inhaling. Relax and lower the buttocks to the floor. Lift again and roll your pelvis slowly around. Repeat 20 times.

independent midwives, may also offer ante-natal classes in your area.

If this is your first baby, then you will probably benefit from attending more than one class. You should receive some useful information on the way your birth is likely to be managed if it is taking place in hospital as well as consideration of your individual emotional needs and more in-depth information on childbirth.

Ante-natal classes are intended to help remove the fear of childbirth caused by

Important

Whilst exercising during pregnancy, you must *never* do sit-ups or lie on your back and raise your legs without bending them.

ignorance. Many women, it is argued, become tense during labour because they do not understand what is happening to them. This makes the pain much worse. By giving women knowledge about childbirth and by

Testing for rectal separation

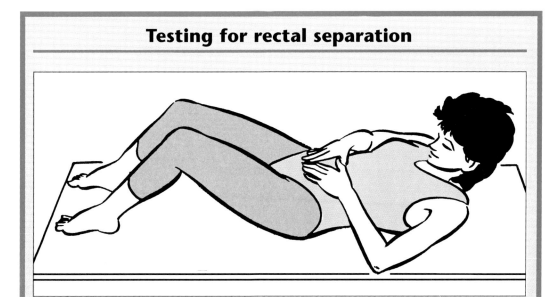

You must be careful when performing any abdominal exercises that you do not separate the rectus muscle. You can test for separation by lying on your back with your knees bent and feet flat on the floor, hip distance apart.

Place your hands on your abdomen with the fingers below the navel. Inhale and slowly lift your head and shoulders off the floor. Rest your chin on your chest as you breathe out again. If the rectal muscle has separated, you will feel the flesh bulging between the muscles.

emphasising that it is a natural process, ante-natal teachers help to give pregnant women a measure of control. They feel that they are no longer timid, passive 'patients.'

The classes also teach you a series of relaxation and breathing exercises to help you deal with the pain and stress of labour. Individual methods vary and some women choose not to use the specific techniques they are taught, but prefer to develop their own for use during labour. Women also learn about specific exercises to help them in childbirth, especially pelvic floor exercises (see opposite).

Classes also bring women together to share worries and experiences and to discuss childbirth and parenthood without the risk of boring their non-pregnant friends. The classes can forge powerful bonds, and often women stay in touch for many years with their fellow ante-natal classmates.

Find out what is available in your area and make sure you book early if you decide to attend privately run classes.

You and your baby: 3 - 6 months

Giving up work

Deciding when to stop working full-time and whether to return to work after having your baby requires careful consideration. Many factors will influence your decision, including your financial situation.

Increasing numbers of women are managing to negotiate a part-time return to work, which can combine the best of both worlds. Others manage to arrange job shares. Talk to your personnel officer or employer about the different possibilities before you make a final decision.

You don't have to make up your mind yet whether to return to work. Some women who feel sure that they will stay at home with their babies still give notice of their intention to return in case they change their minds or have to return to work earlier than expected for financial reasons. This may damage your relationship with your employer, however, making it difficult to arrange a return at a later date.

Being at home with a baby can be very different from your expectations. Some women are surprised to find that they enjoy it far more than they imagined and cannot bear the thought of returning; others find it boring and stifling and need the outside stimulus of a job. If you do decide to give up work, try to keep in touch with your former workplace and colleagues. Try to visit them occasionally and arrange to meet up socially from time to time. This will help to keep doors open for you when and if the time arrives at which you do wish to return to the world of work.

Time off work

If you are working full-time in the UK, remember that you are entitled to time off for ante-natal check-ups.

Childcare

If you are thinking of returning to work, full or part-time, organising good childcare for your baby is essential. You have to feel happy and confident with the arrangements you have made for caring for your baby, otherwise it is impossible to concentrate at work and the whole situation becomes unbearably stressful.

Start to find out about childcare services

in your area. In the UK, there are local registered childminders, and your town council should have a list of people in your area. Many working mothers have forged very successful links with childminders and if you manage to find someone warm, caring and trustworthy you will know your baby is in excellent hands. You could also discuss the possibility of a friend or relative looking

Action plan

1 Investigate your local and mail order maternity wear shops. You need to buy two or three well-fitted maternity bras and a selection of clothes to see you through to the end of your pregnancy. Maternity hire shops hire out clothes for special occasions.

2 Find out about the ante-natal tests routinely offered in your area. If you want others, inform your doctor.

3 Investigate the range of local ante-natal classes available and book yourself (and maybe your partner too) into a course.

4 Find out about the range of maternity benefits and think about when you want to give up work.

5 Consider your options regarding working after the baby is born. You may want to discuss these with your employer.

6 Find out about childcare options.

7 Check your diet. Now that your feelings of nausea have disappeared, you may be tempted to eat less healthy foods.

after your baby, particularly if you share similar views on caring for and bringing up children.

Ask friends who work what arrangements they have made for their children. A nanny could be an option if you are planning to return to work full-time, but they are expensive. Some mothers manage to share a nanny and thereby halve the cost. A mother's help is another alternative if you are planning to work just a few hours or if you are able to work from home. These are often mums with older children, looking for part-time work themselves whilst their children are at school. Look in your local telephone directory for nanny agencies, as they often have mother's helps on their books too.

Some day nurseries do care for young babies, but research has shown that these are often not ideal environments for very young children, even though they may look very smart and professional.

Your baby's development: 3-6 months

As we have already seen, your baby is fully developed by the end of the twelfth week of pregnancy. For the remaining 28 weeks it has to grow and mature, and this process is very important to enable it to live independently outside the womb in the future.

By 24 weeks your baby has its own legal rights. Babies as young as 22 weeks have survived but they are the exceptions. At 26 weeks the survival rate is 50 per cent. The main problems are the immaturity of the lungs – unlike other organs they do not work

You and your baby: 3 - 6 months

until after the baby is born – and the lack of temperature control. Very premature babies have very little fat on their bodies.

Weeks 13 - 16

The baby has plenty of room to move about in the amniotic sac which cushions and protects it in the womb. Although the baby is now growing rapidly, it is still small enough to fit into a teacup! It is covered with fine, downy hair, called lanugo. This even covers its face. The sexual organs continue to develop and the sex of the baby is now obvious. All the joints are formed.

Weeks 17 - 20

By the 20th week you should have felt your baby move. At first it feels like a fluttering inside your stomach but gradually the movements become stronger and more like kicks or punches. This is because its muscles are developing rapidly, enabling it to make very active movements. The baby also starts to produce vernix, a creamy white substance that protects it from the amniotic fluid. The eyes are still closed and appear large and widely spaced, as the face is not yet rounded out. The baby is 25.5cms/10 inches long.

Weeks 20 - 24

Your baby's hearing has developed. It can hear your heart beating, the blood rushing through your system and loud noises and music. It may even start to recognise the sound of your voice.

The baby is still rather thin, as fatty deposits have not yet been laid down, but its muscles are now fully developed.

Weeks 24 - 28

A baby born at 28 weeks has a 90 per cent chance of survival in the best intensive care units. The main difficulty is that it has not yet developed bubbles of surfactant, a substance that prevents the lungs from collapsing each time it breathes. Some intensive care baby units are now giving premature babies artificial surfactant and it is hoped that this will reduce significantly the number of babies dying or damaged by lack of oxygen.

The baby's head has grown more than its body so it looks more in proportion. At 28 weeks, it is 37cm/15 inches long.

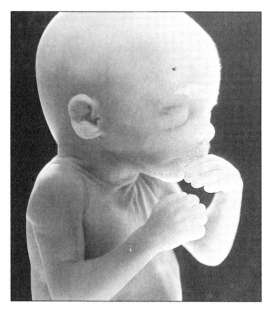

This fetus is around five months old and now looks like a human being! You can see that the face is formed, and the fingers even have tiny nails. It is still growing rapidly in weight and length, and the muscles are developing and getting stronger.

Months 3-6

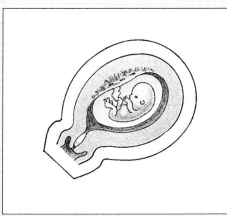

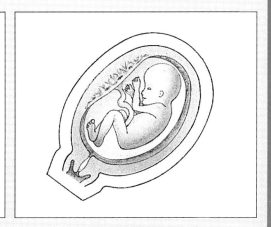

During the middle trimester of pregnancy, the fetus grows rapidly. By month six, the fetus will look much as it will at birth, although it lacks fat beneath the skin and therefore looks quite thin and wrinkled. Inside the womb, its ears are functioning and it is getting used to noises from the outside world as well as the sounds of your heart beating and your stomach rumbling.

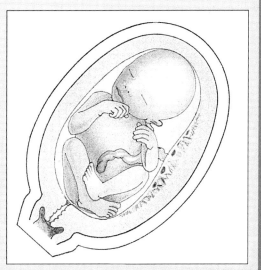

The amniotic fluid in which the baby is suspended is renewed constantly and acts as a shock absorber to protect it. If you bump into something or fall over, you are unlikely to harm the baby.

By the seventh month of pregnancy, most of the available space in the uterus will be taken up by the baby and it will soon turn into a head-down position in readiness for birth. When this happens, it will fit a little more comfortably.

Chapter four

You and your baby: 6 - 9 months

"I know I've still got a week to go but the waiting is getting monotonous. The baby feels low and puts pressure on my bladder. It seems enormous. I feel quite depressed but don't want to bore everyone."

You may have already finished work, or be about to very soon. Some women feel full of energy and excitement as the birth day draws nearer, but many more feel ambivalent. On the one hand, you want the pregnancy to finish so that your body can get back to 'normal', but at the same time there is a slight feeling of panic about the oncoming labour you have to go through first.

You have probably been looking forward to having time at home to yourself, yet when it arrives you can feel in a strange sort of limbo. Your past life is over but your new life as a family has not yet begun.

Make sure you plan something for every day so that you get out of the house, but allow time to rest, too. Visit friends, enjoy a walk in the park, go to the cinema, to a concert or on a shopping trip. A trip to your ante-natal exercise and relaxation class will also break up the day and give you a chance to meet people. Spoil yourself in these last weeks of freedom – and don't feel guilty about it! They will pass more quickly and you will enjoy the waiting time.

Get organised

You need to get organised on a practical level. It is important that you have prepared somewhere to put all the baby's things. You may be able to use the spare room, although you will probably find it easier if he sleeps in your room for the first few weeks. You need to collect the essential clothes and equipment you will need.

Try to stock up the freezer, too; cooking and storing food now will help you in the early weeks after the birth when you will not have the same amount of time and energy to prepare and cook meals, and there are constant interruptions.

Buy a good childcare book and ask friends with children for tips and advice on coping with a small baby. If you live in the UK, you can always ask your local Health Visitor for advice – one of her main functions is to support families with new babies.

Your health

When you consider the enormous changes taking place inside your body, it is hardly surprising that you feel some discomfort or irritation during pregnancy. The following problems can occur at any time but they are often most troublesome during the last few weeks before the baby is born. Here is some practical advice on how to avoid them.

Backache

Your body tissues and ligaments are softening, whilst the amount of weight you are carrying increases. If your stomach muscles are not strong enough to support this extra weight, your back muscles will become strained. Towards the end of your pregnancy you may start to tip your weight backwards in an effort to balance.

Tips to avoid backache

- Try to stand straight with your pelvis tucked in: imagine you are carrying a book on your head!
- Always wear low-heeled shoes.
- Sit in a straight-backed chair with a small cushion or rolled-up towel in the hollow of your spine. Sit to do household jobs like cooking and ironing.
- Sit cross-legged whenever you can, keeping your back straight.
- Bend your knees when lifting, do *not* bend from the waist.
- To get out of bed, roll on to your side first and push yourself up using your arm muscles for support.
- Sleep on a firm mattress. If yours is soft, then ask your partner to put a piece of hardboard underneath it.
- To rest your back, get down on to all-fours as often as possible. Try this exercise.

Get on all-fours with your hands and knees apart. Round your back upwards, like a cat, and tuck your head into your chest, feeling the stretch through your whole body. Lift your head and relax your back. Repeat.

You and your baby: 6-9 months

Bladder problems

During late (and early) pregnancy you need to pass water more often. In late pregnancy this is caused by pressure on the bladder from the baby's head pressing on it.

Tips to avoid bladder problems

- If you have to get up in the night try cutting out late evening drinks, although it is important to drink plenty during the day (see constipation below).
- Some women find that it helps to rock backwards and forwards whilst they pass water, lessening the pressure on the bladder so that they can empty it more completely.
- Contact your doctor if you have pain or blood when passing urine.
- Doing your pelvic floor exercises every day will help you avoid problems.

Constipation

This is caused by hormones in your body relaxing the walls of your intestine, and making it more difficult to expel the contents. It may be made worse by the weight of the uterus and the growing baby exerting additional pressure on the bowel. Your best protection against constipation is to eat a healthy diet which supplies plenty of high-fibre fresh fruit, vegetables and whole-grain cereals. Fibre is indigestible, retains water and gives bulk to food. It helps waste products to move more quickly through the bowel for elimination. A high-fibre diet will help keep you regular.

Tips to avoid constipation

- You should drink at least two litres of fluid every day.
- Open your bowels as soon as you feel the urge, however inconvenient.
- Eat plenty of fibre – fruit, vegetables, beans, lentils, whole-grain bread and cereals
- Exercise regularly to keep your muscles toned up.
- Avoid taking iron pills if possible. If you are taking them and they make your constipation worse, ask your doctor if you can change to a different type.

Indigestion and heartburn

You may find that foods you usually enjoy give you indigestion during pregnancy. Heartburn is a searing pain which is felt in the lower part of the chest. You may also bring up small quantities of sour, acidy fluid. Heartburn is caused by the relaxation of the stomach valve, allowing acid to pass into the oesophagus or food pipe. It is made worse by the growing uterus pushing against the stomach.

Tips for indigestion

- Try to eat smaller portions more often. 'Graze' throughout the day on small healthy snacks rather than eating three large meals.

- Always sit up straight whilst eating.

Tips for heartburn

- Tell your doctor if you experience heartburn. He will be able to prescribe some safe medication for you.

- Many women find that milk of magnesia or a glass of milk are often effective in relieving heartburn, but do not swallow too large a quantity or your stomach will compensate by producing even more acid.

- If heartburn troubles you at night, take a glass of milk before going to bed, and sleep well propped up with several pillows. Avoid eating carbohydrates in the evening.

Piles (haemorrhoids)

Piles are swollen veins either just inside or outside the anus. They can feel very uncomfortable and may bleed when you open your bowels.

Hormonal changes during pregnancy relax the blood vessels, and the pressure of the baby's head may cause an obstruction in the blood supply. Piles are made worse by constipation and straining to open your bowels. Occasionally, piles get worse during labour but they usually subside after delivery.

Thrombosed piles

A thrombosed pile containing a blood clot is one of the most painful conditions to occur during pregnancy. Walking or sitting down will be most uncomfortable. There are ointments to alleviate the symptoms. The thrombosed pile should subside after several days.

43

You and your baby: 6-9 months

Tips to ease the pain of piles

- If the piles stick out after you open your bowels, push them gently back inside with your finger. If this is difficult, try lying in a warm bath for a few minutes.
- Tell your doctor if you have piles – he may prescribe a soothing ointment – or if you experience rectal bleeding.
- Witch hazel or a pack of crushed ice (or a packet of frozen peas) covered with a cloth helps to ease the discomfort. You can also buy special creams and lotions from the pharmacist or your local drugstore.
- Try not to get constipated. Eat a high-fibre diet. You can buy special high-fibre drinks from your chemist or drugstore to encourage soft and regular bowel movements until the soreness has passed.
- If you suffer from piles discuss this with your doctor before you become pregnant again. They may become worse during each pregnancy and it is possible to have them treated.

Swelling of legs, ankles, fingers (oedema)

Your body holds more water than usual during pregnancy. At the end of the day, particularly if you have been standing for long periods or the weather is particularly hot, water tends to gather in the lower parts of the body and your ankles swell.

Tips for avoiding swelling

- Avoid standing and rest on your bed for an hour or two each day, with your feet raised above your head.
- Try these exercises: rotate one foot 10 times clockwise followed by 10 times anti-clockwise. Repeat with the other foot. Stretch and bend each foot 25 times. You can do this several times a day: at the office, sitting down in the evening, or when travelling on the train or in the car.
- If you experience any swelling always tell your midwife or doctor.

Varicose veins

These are common in pregnancy and are caused by the hormone progesterone relaxing the muscles of the vein walls and making them stretch. Varicose veins are made worse by long periods of standing, putting on a lot of weight and, in later pregnancy, by the uterus pressing on veins in the pelvis. This obstructs the flow of blood from the legs to the heart, thus increasing pressure on the veins in the legs. Sore or itchy skin above a vein or a dull, aching pain in the calf are early warning signs.

Tips for varicose veins

- Try to avoid excessive weight gain.
- Do not stand for long periods.
- Do not cross your legs.
- Make sure you take regular exercise.
- Sit with your legs propped up on a stool.
- Do not wear tight stockings, tights (panty hose) or underwear that constrict the top of the legs.
- Buy several pairs of support tights (panty hose) from your chemist and wear them continuously.
- Occasionally varicose veins can occur in the vulva, causing itching and irritation. They usually disappear after delivery; if not, a simple operation will get rid of them.

Bridging exercise

1 Lie down with some cushions to support your head and shoulders, arms at your sides and feet raised on a box or stool. 2 Pull in and tighten your buttocks and pelvic floor muscles and, keeping your back straight, slowly lift your lower back off the floor. Hold for a count of 10 and then lower. Repeat the exercise 10 times.

You and your baby: 6-9 months

Stretch marks

Some women get them; others do not. They are caused by a combination of an increase in progesterone, rapid weight gain and fluid retention. Stretch marks usually occur on the breasts and abdomen. Creams and oils do little to prevent them but may help relieve itchiness. Stretch marks fade from ugly red marks to pale silvery streaks after delivery, but they never disappear completely. A good diet may help to prevent them.

Your baby's development: 6-9 months

Weeks 28 - 32

The baby is perfectly formed, lacking only a layer of insulating fat and some surfactant. Movements are strongly felt by you, and you may also be aware of an occasional attack of hiccups if the baby has been gulping too much amniotic fluid! It is 40.5cm/16 inches long.

Weeks 32 - 36

Around 36 weeks the baby's head may 'engage' in the pelvis. This means that it has moved down ready to be born and is a sign that the pelvis is big enough for the baby to pass through.

Once this has happened you should find that you can breathe more easily but sitting can be uncomfortable and your body may feel 'low slung'. If the baby is a boy, then the testicles will have descended into the scrotum. It is now 46cm/18½ inches long.

Kick chart

During the last few weeks of pregnancy your midwife may ask you to fill in a kick chart. This monitors the baby's movements inside your uterus. Sometimes the chart requires you to note down the times of 10 or 12 movements within a 24-hour period. By now you should recognise your baby's pattern of movement. If it seems very still for a 24-hour period you should contact your midwife or doctor immediately.

Important

If you suffer from any of the following, contact your doctor immediately:
- Vaginal bleeding.
- A leak of fluid from the vagina.
- Sudden swelling of your face, hands or feet.
- Discoloured or smelly vaginal discharge.
- High fever.
- Severe dizziness.
- Acute shortness of breath.
- Excessive vomiting.
- No fetal movements felt for 24 hours.
- Severe abdominal pain.

Months 7-9

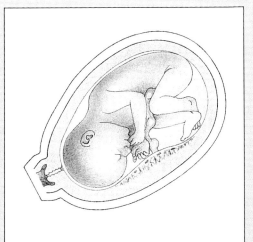

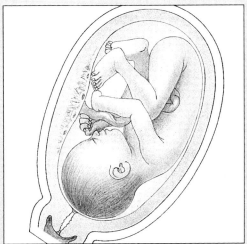

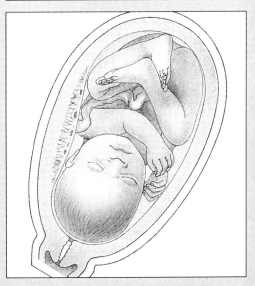

At seven months (above) your baby starts to look fatter, and would probably survive if born prematurely. It now weighs around 2kg/4lb and is covered with waxy vernix to protect its delicate skin. By month 8 (above right), it is fully formed although it still needs to grow a little more. It is starting to get cramped inside the womb as the baby has now filled nearly all the available space. Its feet turn slightly inwards and the legs are bent at the hips and knees and crossed. The arms are folded too.

As the birth draws nearer the baby settles down lower in your pelvis (right) and engages ready for the big moment. It practises its breathing movements and may even get hiccups! It is now ready to start its journey through the birth canal into the outside world.

The average baby weighs about 3.4kg/7lb at birth and may be born any time between the thirty eighth and forty second weeks.

Chapter five

Getting ready for birth

Buying baby clothes and equipment

Walking into a babycare shop can seem an overwhelming experience. As you look at the rows of beautiful clothes and the shelves of bright and gleaming equipment you may wonder where to start. Do you really need all these goods to bring up a baby? If not, how do you know what is best to choose?

Elegant layettes and outfits for every occasion certainly look appealing but they are expensive, may be impractical and are definitely not necessary. In the early weeks your baby will need to feel warm and

---

Essentials

- Six babygro stretch suits – or four stretch suits and two nighties. Although nighties can 'ruck up', they do allow air to circulate around the baby's body so he can cool off if he gets too hot. Avoid leaving long ties which are very dangerous if they wrap up around the baby's throat.
- Four vests – cotton if it is summer; thermal if it is winter. All-in-one bodysuits fasten between the legs so there is no awkward gap around the tummy.
- Two/three cardigans – wool is most comfortable and not too heavy (several light layers of clothes are preferable to one heavy one).
- Two pairs of mittens – one pair should be wool to wear outside if it's cold; the second pair should be cotton to leave on your baby during the first week or two if he scratches his face when he is sleeping.
- Woolly hat and bootees – for going out in cold weather.
- Socks – to wear under his nightie. Do not put socks over a babygro suit.
- Sunhat to protect your baby's head and eyes if it is summer.
- A shawl or blanket to wrap your baby in – choose close-knitted patterns so that his fingers do not get caught.

---

comfortable; it should not be constricted by uncomfortable, itchy headbands or irritated by fussy bootees he cannot remove. Only the minimum of first-sized clothes are needed as babies quickly grow out of them. Indeed some large babies never fit into the smallest sizes!

Nappies (diapers)

You need to decide whether you are going to use terry towelling or disposable nappies. If you can afford the extra cost, disposable ones save an awful lot of work. You have no worries about drying them either.

Some environmentalists argue against disposable nappies but other experts assert that terries are not a perfect alternative. Washing powders are not all biodegradable and the extra washing and tumble drying uses up a lot of electricity. Terries can be awkward to use at first, particularly on small babies, and leakage may result.

The large economy packs of disposable nappies are the cheapest, but the branded names are often more reliable. Provided that you buy the right size you should feel very confident about using them and not have to worry at all about leakage.

If you decide to use terry nappies you will need the following items:
● 24 nappies.
● Disposable nappy liners.
● Nappy pins.
● Four pairs of plastic pants.
● Sterilizing powder or liquid.
● Nappy bucket with lid.
For changing nappies you will need:
● Cotton wool – rolls are cheaper than balls.
● Baby lotion or baby wipes (water is fine

> ## Important
> Nappy sacks are handy for disposing of used nappies but always keep them high up out of your baby's reach. One baby died when he leaned over his cot and managed to pick one up.

but these are handy to have, particularly when you are away from home).
● Nappy rash cream.
● Changing mat.
● Changing bag to keep everything in.

The safest place to change a baby is on the floor. If you get into this habit from the start you will not be tempted to use a higher surface when your baby is older and can roll off. Even very young babies can suddenly surprise you with a new movement. If you do use a high surface for changing nappies you must *never* leave your baby – not even for a second. He could roll and fall.

Equipment

Buying everything new for your baby is a tremendous expense, especially as some items only last for a few months. Ask your midwife about baby equipment hire schemes operating in your area. If you do hire or buy second-hand, check the equipment very carefully. All fixings must be secure, with no loose parts. Items you might consider hiring include the following items:
● Baby sling.
● Travel cot – for weekends away.
● Travelling high chair – for babies of seven months plus.

Getting ready for birth

- Backpack – for babies of nine months plus.
- First car seat – from birth to nine months.
- Pram – until your baby is six weeks old and can go in a pushchair or buggy.
- Bouncing cradle – from two weeks to four months.
- Crib – for your newborn baby to sleep in

If you are buying new equipment check that it complies with safety regulations. You will need the following essentials.

Somewhere to sleep

For 3-4 months your baby can sleep in a crib, carrycot or Moses basket. He should be close to you, preferably in your room. Make sure that he has a well-fitted safety mattress with no gaps around the side to trap his head. The mattress should have a plastic cover with holes in to allow air to circulate.

At four months (earlier if your baby is big) he will need to move into a cot. Choose this piece of equipment carefully, as you will use it for at least two years. Again, check that the mattress fits snugly. If you decide to buy, borrow or hire a second-hand cot, it is worth investing in a new mattress if you can possibly afford it. If not, then clean the old mattress scrupulously. If the cot is second-hand you must also check that the paint or varnish is non-toxic and that there are no splinters or loose parts on it.

Make sure the cot bars are secure and close together (they should be no more than 60mm/2½ inches apart and no less than 25mm/1 inch). Choose one with a drop side so you can lift your baby in and out easily, but make sure there is a safety catch so that he cannot undo it too.

Cot bumpers look appealing but the ties can wrap round your baby's neck. They can also obscure your vision of the baby. If you want to use one, secure it firmly with short strings and remove it once your baby is active.

Bedding

You need four light blankets and six sheets. Three could be fitted to cover the mattress but you can also use unfitted ones. You could cut up your own old cotton sheets to make some for your baby. Follow this guide to decide how much bedding to use:

15°C/60°F – sheet plus four layers of blanket

18°C/65°F – sheet plus three to four layers of blanket

21°C/70°F – sheet plus two to three layers of blanket

24°C/75°F – sheet plus one layer of blanket

27°C/80°F – sheet only

This guide assumes that your baby is wearing a babygro, nappy and vest. If your baby is hot, remove a layer of bedding.

Do not use a duvet or pillow until your baby is at least one year old. Avoid baby nests and sheepskins. It is very important not to overwrap your baby, particularly in the winter months when many parents add extra layers even though the temperature is warm inside the home.

Thermometer

It is worth investing in a wall-hanging thermometer so that you can check the temperature of the room in which the baby is sleeping – particularly when he is new-born. The ideal room temperature for your baby is 18°C/65°F.

Bathing

All you need is a large plastic bowl. Many sophisticated bath 'aids' are on the market but they are totally unnecessary and just clutter up the bathroom. Indeed, some, such as those which are fitted with special support seats, may encourage you to let go of your baby and this can be very dangerous.

In an emergency you can use a sink, but tie a towel round both taps before you put your baby in. You will also need baby soap or baby bath liquid and two soft towels kept just for your baby. If your baby has dry skin, you can rub in a little baby oil.

Transport

You will need something in which your baby can travel. Your options include:

● **A baby sling** This enables you to carry your baby in front of you, leaving your hands free. Check that there is good head and neck support for your baby. Your baby will love it, as he is warm from your body heat and close to you. Most small babies will sleep very contentedly in baby slings, rocked to sleep by the warmth and your walking movement. Baby slings are ideal for small babies but they do put a strain on your shoulders and are very tiring to wear once your baby has reached three or four months.

● **A pushchair** Use this in conjunction with a sling, as you must not put a baby in a pushchair until he is at least six weeks old. (Some models do adjust so that your baby can lie completely flat and the manufacturers say these can be used with newborn babies). You will also need a hood and apron for wet weather and a sunshade for use in summer.

Lightweight buggies are easy to store and useful for public transport but you must not use them with babies younger than six months. As they do not recline they can be uncomfortable for babies to sleep in.

● **A carrycot on wheels** This is versatile and can be transported in a car. The baby sleeps in the carrycot inside and can be taken out by using the wheels.

● **Car seat/restraints** If you are using a carrycot in your car, proper restraints are essential. You may need to get them fitted at a garage by a trained fitter.

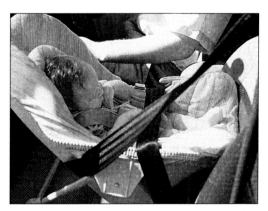

● **A pram** Very spacious and comfortable for your baby but it cannot be transported easily and storage could be a problem. You will need a pram harness.

● **Three-in-one transporter** This converts from a pram and carrycot into a pushchair as your baby grows older.

Getting ready for birth

Other equipment

● **Bouncing chair/cradle** A handy chair for a young baby, as he can sit supported and watch your movements. You should never put a bouncing chair or cradle on a worktop and stop using it once your baby starts to roll over or sit up unaided.

Most experts agree that a rear-facing front car seat is safer for a young baby than a front-facing seat or carrycot restraint. If you decide to buy a car seat you will need to choose between different types. Some are designed to be used for babies from 0-9 months; others can be used from 0-4 years. A third category is designed for babies from six months to four years. Lightweight polystyrene seats are easy to carry, and studies have shown that many parents fail to fit heavy, metal-framed seats correctly. Although these are supposed to fit into an adult belt, in practice many do not.

Packing your suitcase

If you have opted for a hospital birth, you will need to have a small suitcase packed three weeks before your due date. You can, of course, add perishable items later. It is best to be prepared well in advance, rather than having to pack a bag once the contractions have begun. Your basic kit should include the following:
● Two or three front-opening nighties.
● Two or three nursing bras if you are breastfeeding or ordinary bras if not.
● Dressing gown.
● Slippers.
● Washbag and toiletries.
● Five or six old pairs of pants or disposable ones.
● 24-30 extra-absorbent sanitary towels.
● Change for telephone or phone card.
● Telephone numbers of friends and relatives.
● Book and/or personal stereo.
● Vaseline for dry lips.

● Sponge for use during labour.
● Thermos of ice cubes to suck during labour.
● Camera for your partner to use.
● Snack for your partner.
● Fruit juice and herb teas.
● Glucose tablets.
● Water spray for moistening face.
● Soft lavatory paper.
● Calendula cream for sore nipples or a sore perineum.
● Hand mirror to watch your baby being born.
● Socks in case your legs and feet get cold.

Note: You might also consider taking in a bucket. Some women find this useful to sit on during the first stage of labour.

For your baby you will need some clothes and a shawl to bring him home in. Check with the hospital if you have to supply your own nappies.

Breathing exercises

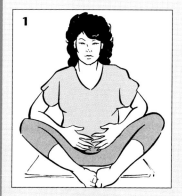

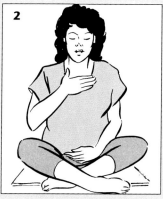

1 Practise these breathing exercises for labour, either 'tailor sitting' (as shown) or cross-legged. Keep your back straight and feet pressed together. Place both hands on your abdomen and inhale through your nose. Exhale through your nose or mouth, trying to relax your abdominal muscles. As you inhale, you should feel your abdomen moving out; as you exhale, it should relax.

2 Practise panting for dealing with the peak of a contraction. Quicker breathing in

shallower breaths will help you surmount the pain. Then ease down gradually into slower, more rhythmic breathing as the contraction subsides. You will feel your upper chest moving under your hand. Breathe in and out quickly two or three times, then sigh and pant again.

3 Practise breathing through a contraction with your hands resting lightly on your knees. Try to feel your chest rising and falling, and relax your abdominal muscles.

Getting ready for birth

Birth plan

During your ante-natal care your midwife may have suggested that you write a birth plan. If not, ask if you can compile one with her help. By now you will have found out a lot about the choices available to you in childbirth and this is a way of recording what you want to happen.

However, if you are having a home birth or using a domino scheme you may feel your midwife knows your preferences and there is no need to make a written record.

Your written birth plan might include the following:
1 Who you wish to be with you during labour.
2 Any special equipment or facilities you would like (birthing chair, beanbags etc.).

Breathing for contractions

1

Contraction

30 seconds → time

1 Gentle contractions before leaving for hospital. Breathe easily and rhythmically with the contractions, not too deep nor too fast. Try to relax into the contractions.

2

Contraction

45 seconds → time

2 As the contractions increase in strength. Breathe faster and more shallow in the upper part of the chest at the peak of the contraction when relaxation is difficult.

3

Contraction

in in in

out

sigh

1 minute 30 seconds → time

3 At the end of the first stage of labour. When contractions become more intense and longer, breathe in groups of three: in-out, in-out, in-sigh. Panting may help if you are not yet fully dilated.

3 How you wish your baby's heart to be monitored.
4 What pain relief, if any, you want to try.
5 Whether you wish to be active and move freely around during labour.
6 How you wish your baby to be delivered.

7 How you wish to feed your baby.
8 Any special concerns or worries you have.
It is a good idea to get your midwife or doctor to sign your birth plan and attach it to your notes, so it can be read by whoever is attending you. Keep your own copy too.

Feeding your baby

During these last few weeks you need to decide whether you plan to breast- or bottle-feed your baby. If you haven't made up your mind, talk to your health visitor or midwife. If you decide to breastfeed you will need two or three nursing bras and a supply of breast pads. Buy the bras when you are about 30 weeks pregnant.

Most experts agree that breastfeeding is best for your baby, although most babies also thrive on formula milk provided that you are scrupulously hygienic in its preparation. Breastfeeding your baby provides immunity against disease and infection and protection against allergies such as asthma and eczema. In fact, breast milk is perfectly tailored to your baby's digestive system, changing its consistency as your baby is more or less hungry. It is cheap, 'on tap' and requires no preparation.

Even if you breastfeed for just a few days you will have provided colostrum for your baby. This rich and creamy substance is produced by your breasts before the milk comes in. It lines your baby's gut and helps protect it against bacteria.

Some breastfeeding mothers find they have problems with sore or cracked nipples whilst the milk supply gets established but these problems do not last long. Others may complain that they feel very tired, as breastfed babies may need to feed more frequently and no one else can help. One solution is to express 'spare' breast milk into a bottle so that your partner can feed the baby occasionally.

You may decide gradually to change to formula milk, particularly if you are planning to return to work. If you are not sure, it is easier to start off with breastfeeding and then change over later on – it is very difficult to stimulate the milk supply if you started with bottlefeeding.

Recent research has shown that babies who were breastfed for 13 weeks or more, with or without added bottle milk or solid food, had much less gastro-intestinal illness than those who were bottlefed from birth. This immunity continued after breastfeeding had stopped.

If you plan to bottlefeed your baby, you must buy six bottles with teats and caps, some sterilizing equipment, a bottle brush and powdered formula milk.

Chapter six

The birth

Many women worry about knowing when labour has started. There are several clear indications that labour is underway and that you are on the final stage of your journey into parenthood. Once labour has begun you will probably feel a sense of excitement, coupled with determination. You have been preparing to face this great challenge for months; now the moment has arrived for your baby's entry into the world.

The signs that labour is beginning

1 Regular painful contractions

You will probably have been experiencing 'practice', or 'Braxton Hicks', contractions for several months, as your abdomen tightens and then relaxes. At the onset of labour these contractions start to come more regularly and to feel uncomfortable. The sensation is like a belt tightening around your back, which spreads round underneath the baby. The contractions should last longer each time (40 seconds or more) and occur at decreasing intervals.

2 A 'show'

Throughout pregnancy a plug of mucous seals the top of the vagina, preventing any infection from entering the uterus. Sometimes the plug comes away before the contractions start and you will notice a 'show', i.e. mucous mixed with blood. It is a sign that some activity is underway but it can still be several days before you go into proper labour. In other labours, contractions are well established before the mucous plug is finally expelled from the vagina.

> # Important
>
> If you are bleeding heavily it is an emergency and you must contact your midwife immediately. It may be a sign that there is something seriously wrong with the placenta and fast action must be taken to ensure your and your baby's safety.

3 Waters breaking

This occurs when the amniotic sac which surrounds the baby is punctured by the pressure from the baby's head and fluid leaks out. It can be a sudden gush or a slow trickle. If this happens, you should contact your community midwife or the hospital. You will probably be told to go in straight away.

Ready for birth

If this is your second or subsequent baby, the head may not engage until the fortieth week. Some babies are ready to be born before their due date; others do not arrive and are said to be 'overdue'. Both types of birth are perfectly normal. You are 85 per cent likely to deliver within 14 days either side of your estimated delivery date.

The baby cannot move as freely now, although you will still feel its legs and arms. In addition you may feel the head pressing down onto your pelvic floor. This can feel quite uncomfortable at times.

The lanugo has disappeared but traces may remain on the shoulders, arms and legs. The lungs are now mature and the body has laid down stores of fat.

You feel tired and heavy; an average newborn baby weighs 3.4kg/7lb. You have nurtured that new life from the moment of conception but now the moment is fast approaching when labour will start and the long wait will be over.

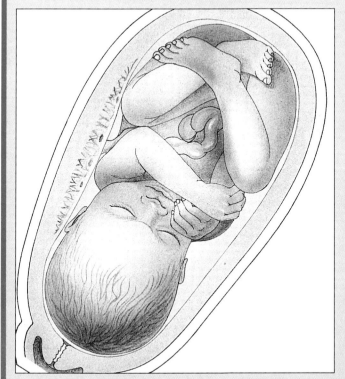

Your baby is ready for birth. It does not move very much because there is very little room to do so. It has now filled out and takes up all the available space.

The birth

Once the waters have broken the baby is no longer protected against infection and there is a chance that the umbilical cord may descend into the birth canal, as it is no longer buoyant. If this happens your baby's oxygen supply may become constricted as the contractions squeeze the cord. During the last few weeks of pregnancy you could protect your bed with a plastic sheet in case the waters break during the night.

Other warning signs

These signs include nausea, diarrhoea and backache. Sometimes you may even feel uncomfortable tightenings for 24 hours or more before labour is established. This may be the cervix gradually ripening and shortening. It can be a sign that your baby is lying with its back to your back. These tightenings occur as it rotates round so that it is in the right position for birth.

During labour your cervix has to dilate to 10cm/4 inches so that the baby can pass through it into your vagina. Labour is said to be established and underway once it has reached 3cm/1¼ inches.

Dilation of the cervix

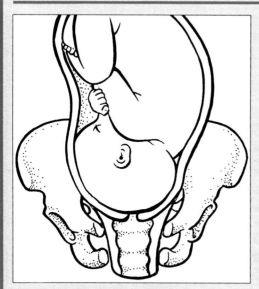 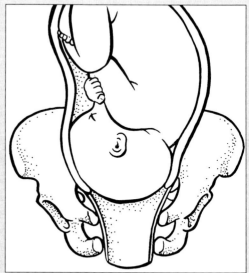

These illustrations show the dilation of the cervix during labour. It is dilated 2cm in the above illustration and the time it takes to reach full dilation (above right) of 10cm varies. Some women take hours to reach 6cm; others are much quicker and may even be 3 or 4cm dilated before they realise that their labour has started.

When to go into hospital

Once contractions are occurring every 10-15 minutes you should phone the hospital or inform your midwife. If you have a long distance to travel to hospital, remember to allow for this.

Many women find they cope well at home in their own surroundings during the early stages of labour. Try to keep upright and active; this helps your baby's head to press down equally on the cervix so that it opens more quickly. A warm bath is relaxing and helps to ease discomfort. Try to eat a nourishing snack – yogurt, muesli, fruit and nuts, cheese or whole-grain bread. If you cannot face a meal, suck some glucose tablets to boost your energy levels.

Contact your partner so that he can be with you and give you moral support and encouragement. You may want to lean over a high-backed chair during the contractions.

You and your partner should pack the final items – ice cubes, sandwiches etc. – in your suitcase before you leave for the hospital. Remember to telephone and let them know that you are on your way.

Arriving at hospital

When you arrive you should go to the admissions desk. An attendant will inform the labour ward and a porter or midwife will accompany you there. Once you are there you will change into a nightdress and the midwife will examine you. This examination will include the following:

● Taking your temperature, pulse and blood pressure and monitoring your urine.
● Listening to your baby's heartbeat.
● Doing an internal examination to see how far your cervix has dilated.

Types of labour

All labours have to progress through the following three main stages:

1 During the first stage the cervix dilates to 10cm to allow the baby's head and body to pass through.
2 During the second stage the baby is pushed through the vagina and delivered.
3 In the third stage the placenta detaches from the uterus and is expelled.

Yet despite this common pattern every woman's experience of labour is different. One factor that can affect the type of labour you experience is the position in which your baby is lying. When the baby is head down to either left or right (left is the most usual position) and curled up, the uterus can work to maximum efficiency, provided the pelvis is big enough to let the baby pass through it. If the baby is lying in a breech position, with its bottom or even a foot presenting first, then the labour may be more drawn out and less straightforward.

As already stated, your baby may be lying with its back to your back, again tipped slightly towards the left or right. This can also make labour more lengthy and cause continual backache throughout. It is very important to empty your bladder regularly

The birth

The progress through the birth canal

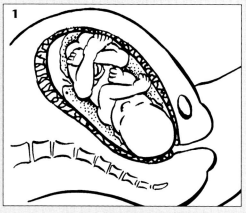

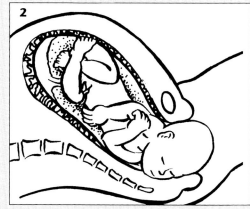

1 The cervix is almost completely dilated towards the end of the first stage of labour. When it reaches 9-10cm, you will get the urge to bear down and push your baby out.
2 In the second stage of labour you have to work hard to push the baby out. Eventually your baby's head will appear in the birth opening with the face turned towards your back.
3 The baby's head emerges and he slides out through the perineum as you push out the shoulders. It is a wonderful sensation to feel your child slithering out of you and to hold him in your arms at last.

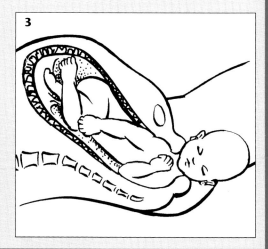

during a long labour and you should also change your position frequently. Squat, go on to all-fours, kneel or sit upright to enable gravity to help you open up and push out your baby. A hot water bottle or some firm massaging pressure on your back can also help to ease the pain of backache.

Some labours are very short and intense. Although this may sound like a desirable state of affairs, in reality it can seem very violent and shocking, as you are thrown right into some fierce and long contractions without a gradual build-up. You will probably find your breathing and relaxation

Positions for labour

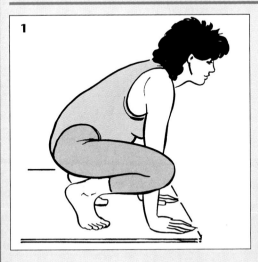

1 Squatting down on your toes and leaning forwards on to your hands for support can help take the weight off your back and helps you work with gravity.

2 You may find it easier to kneel on all-fours. This position is good for preventing or easing backache during labour as it enables the uterus to fall forwards.

The birth

Positions for labour

3 During the first stage of labour you may prefer to use a chair for support. Kneel on the floor in front of the chair with your arms resting on the seat.

4 As labour progresses and the contractions come harder and faster, try leaning forwards on to a chair and resting your head on your arms for support.

5 Alternatively, you can sit the wrong way round on the chair and lean against the back. All the positions illustrated here enable you to stay relatively upright and help speed up your labour.

Note: it is helpful if you practise the various positions shown before the birth so that you can find out which is the most comfortable and relaxing for you. During the first stage of labour, mobility is important and you will probably find it easier if you walk about for as long as possible. When you feel a contraction coming on, you can adopt one of these positions.

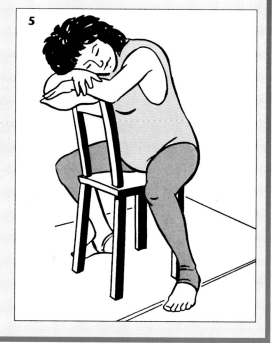

exercises a tremendous boost. Your partner can help you to focus your thoughts and efforts on the techniques you have learnt at ante-natal classes. You may start to shake or feel very cold at the end of the first stage. A pair of long socks packed in your case is useful to keep your feet and legs warm, together with a hot water bottle, until the transition stage between the first and second stages of labour is over.

A long drawn out, stop-and-start labour, by contrast, can be demoralizing and very tiring. Sometimes contractions are uneven, with several strong ones being followed by a series of weak, ineffectual ones. In hospital, doctors may decide to set up an oxytocin drip to speed up your contractions.

Take advantage of the break to have a drink or really relax your body. It is also important not to get dehydrated during a long labour. Another cause of delay is when the cervix does not retract fully from the baby's head and a tiny lip gets stuck. This occurs at the end of the first stage of labour and means you must resist the urge to bear down until the head is free. Short, sharp breaths through contractions are a useful technique for these circumstances.

Caesarean birth

If you are giving birth to a breech baby you will probably be moved into an operating theatre at the end of the first stage in case you need an emergency caesarean. Try not to push during the second stage until the baby is born and the head is about to slip out. The doctor may do an episiotomy (make a cut in your perineum) to ease the passage of the baby's head.

Some non-breech babies are also born by emergency caesarean if you or the baby are at risk. The operation is quick, lasting only 10 minutes, and it can be done under general anaesthetic, or using an epidural so that you will be conscious when your baby is born. You will feel some pulling and a sensation of wetness when the waters break, but a screen will be put across so that you cannot see the operation.

Some women know they are going to have a caesarean in advance. This is called an 'elective' caesarean. Sometimes women are allowed to go through a normal labour for a set time to see if they can deliver vaginally before a decision is taken by the medical staff to perform a caesarean.

Length of labour

On average the first stage of labour is expected to last for 10 hours – one for every centimetre that the cervix dilates. In reality, labour times can vary from six to 12 hours for this first stage. First babies usually take longer than second and subsequent babies to be born.

The birth

Coping with pain

Your midwife or doctor will have discussed the different types of pain relief available and the advantages and drawbacks of each. You may plan to manage with little or no pain relief and to rely on breathing and relaxation techniques. If you reach the end of the first stage and feel you cannot cope much longer, gas and air (entonox) is a useful form of pain relief to get you into the second stage of labour. It does not affect you or the baby and you will be fully conscious

throughout to help push out your baby.
Some women find the pain is too great

Breech birth

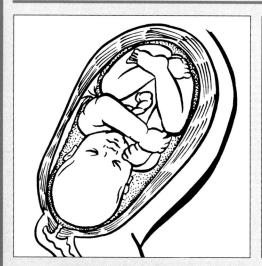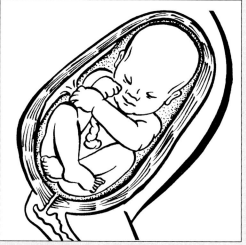

For the uterus to work effectively to open the cervix and push the baby out into the birth canal, the baby should be head down (left). In a breech birth, the baby has not turned and this may in some instances necessitate a caesarean delivery. If possible, the baby will be delivered vaginally with its buttocks slipping out first and then the legs, shoulders and head.

and need something stronger. An injection of pethidine or an epidural anaesthetic are two alternatives. They are both very effective methods of pain relief but they have some disadvantages as well as advantages.

Pethidine can make you feel nauseous and disorientated; an epidural numbs all feeling and pain but you will not be able to get out of bed and you may be unable to feel the second-stage pushing contractions, making a forceps delivery and an episiotomy more likely.

The birth

The second stage of labour progresses much more quickly than the first. The waves of vice-like contractions gradually adapt into an overwhelming desire to bear down and push out your baby. The first indication that you are approaching the second stage is usually a strange, lifting sensation at the base of the spine. You may even find yourself grunting involuntarily, and this is a very exciting moment. Towards the end of the first stage many women feel they have reached the

Your partner can actively help you throughout your labour: helping with your breathing and offering reassurance and support. Get him to rub your back to ease backache in the early stages.

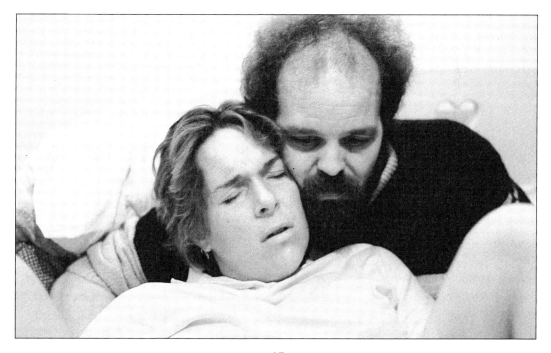

The birth

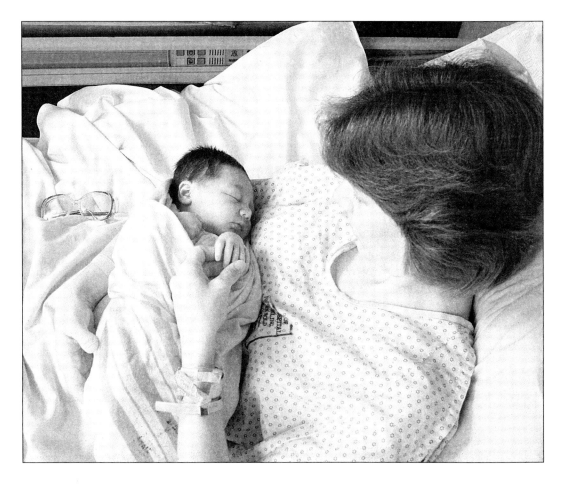

When your baby has been bathed and weighed, he will be handed to you and you can get to know each other at last. If you are planning to breastfeed him, this is a good time to put him on the breast. The nutritious colostrum will come through first. It helps protect your baby against bacteria and infection.

limits of their endurance. Some start to feel panicky; others get increasingly angry and irritable. But once the second stage arrives most women are able to re-focus their energies and find that delivering their baby is one of the most satisfying and moving experiences of their lives.

During the second stage, as the baby's head moves into the vagina, you can reach down to touch it or look at it in a mirror. Once the head is about to be delivered the midwife will tell you to stop pushing and to pant through the next contraction. This gives the perineum time to stretch out gently so the head can be born without tearing your skin. If the perineum will not stretch, the midwife or doctor may make a small cut or episiotomy so the head has room to be born.

Once the baby's head is born, the body slides out with one more push. The midwife will then lift the baby straight onto your tummy before the cord is cut. Once this is done your partner will also be given an opportunity to hold the baby, perhaps after he has been cleaned and wrapped in a blanket.

Between 20 minutes and an hour after your baby is born, the placenta is delivered. You may be given an injection to speed this up and prevent the risk of a haemorrhage if the womb does not contract properly.

If you have a tear or episiotomy you will be sewn up. These stitches will dissolve naturally and need not be removed. A small tear is often left to heal itself.

Your baby will be weighed and measured and given an all-over check. As a result of this, he is given an Apgar score out of ten at one minute and five minutes after birth. This measures muscle tone, skin colour, breathing and general alertness. Most babies score seven and over.

If you are breastfeeding, you will be encouraged to put your baby to the breast as soon as possible. You will probably be amazed at how naturally he 'roots' for the breast and latches on. Sometimes babies seem sleepy after birth and may not be interested immediately. Offer the breast again a little later; ask your midwife to help you.

You and your partner will want to discover your son or daughter together. You need time to meet your baby and welcome him or her into the world. This is a very special moment; ask for more time alone if you feel that you need it.

When things go wrong

Sadly, not every pregnancy ends with a healthy baby, although the overwhelming majority do. Sometimes babies are born early or sick and, instead of being with you, they are treated in special care units.

This can be a devastating experience. The hi-tech equipment can seem frightening and alienating and your baby may look like a tiny, vulnerable stranger.

Staff will explain what each piece of equipment does, and they are also trained to help you come to terms with what is happening. If your baby is very sick you may

be terrified that he may not live. You may also feel angry and upset that you have been 'cheated' out of the normal, healthy baby you had every right to expect.

In these cases it is very important that you establish a bond with your baby, and feeding is one very important way in which you can do this. Expressed breast milk can be fed to your baby through a tube, and you will be shown how you can encourage your milk supply. Touching and talking to your baby is another important way of creating a bond. He knew your voice in the womb; he will find its reassuring sound a comfort in this strange new world.

Four out of every hundred babies are born with some form of handicap. A quarter of these are mild abnormalities that can be easily treated or require no treatment. A further quarter are slightly more serious but will not deter your baby from leading a normal life. Moderate handicaps include hare lips and hip dislocations, both of which can be surgically corrected.

Severe handicap affects one in every hundred babies born. Down's syndrome and cerebral palsy are two examples of severe handicap. There are a number of people who can help if you have a handicapped baby; your pediatrician or doctor should give you information about voluntary and statutory organisations. In the UK, your health visitor can also help in a positive way: she offers support following the birth of a handicapped baby, providing you with information. In these circumstances, she would have an ongoing relationship with your family and be able to put you in touch with other people in a similar position.

In the UK about 8000 parents lose a baby each year, either because they are stillborn or because they die during the first weeks of life. Some of these babies have such serious illnesses that little can be done to help them; others seem fit and healthy and the cause of death may never be known.

If this happens to you, you will probably feel very shocked. You may need to grieve to start to come to terms with such an unimaginable loss. Your suffering may be intense but you may eventually come to a form of acceptance provided that you are encouraged to mourn and express your feelings of devastation, anger and despair.

Holding and naming your baby can be very comforting. A memento, such as a photograph or lock of hair, may also help you to think of him as a real person. You may wish to be involved in a burial service and to have a grave in which to place your baby, or you may prefer not to know where he is buried.

You will want to know why your baby died and will appreciate honest and open information from medical staff. Counselling will probably be essential before you consider another pregnancy. No one needs to tell you that the baby you lost was quite unique and irreplaceable; but subconsciously you may try to bring it back by getting pregnant again very quickly. These are feelings you need to talk through with your partner and whoever is counselling you.

Cot death

Cot death, or Sudden Infant Death Syndrome (SIDS), is the most common cause of death in babies between one month and one year. Extensive research has pointed to four simple steps that parents can take to reduce the risk:

1 **Lie your baby on his back or side to sleep**. Lying face down can cause a baby's upper airways to become restricted. If a baby buries his face in the mattress it prevents heat loss, which is vital to stop him from overheating.

Babies have a well-developed gag reflex

which means they will cough to prevent milk from going down into the lungs.

2 Do not overwrap or overheat your baby. Two-thirds of cot deaths occur during the winter, and it has been documented that some parents wrap their babies more heavily during the winter months, even if the room temperature is the same as in the summer.

New babies need to be kept warm but once they are a month old they do not need any more clothes than an adult indoors, although they should be protected from draughts. Outside they do need extra layers as they are not moving to keep warm.

When indoors, babies should not have their heads covered, and covers on their cot should be left loose so they can shake them off easily if they get too hot.

To check your baby's temperature, feel the back of his neck or his tummy – not hands, which may be outside the bedding and feel cold when the rest of his body is warm.

If your baby is hot, remove a layer of bedding. Babies have died when parents put extra blankets on at night and radiators came on in the morning. It is not usually necessary to keep the heating on all night.

3 Avoid smoking and do not let other people smoke near your baby. If your partner or other members of your family smoke, encourage them to give up.

4 Contact your doctor if your baby is unwell. Many cot death babies, although apparently healthy, turn out to have had minor respiratory infections. Any baby under six months who has a temperature of 38°C for more than two hours should be seen by a doctor.

If your baby has a fever, remove layers of clothing to help him cool down. Sponge him with tepid water – babies over four months can be given liquid paracetamol.

One theory about cot death asserts that old mattresses contain germs that can build up to dangerous levels. Try to buy a new mattress. If you cannot afford to, give your second-hand one a thorough cleaning. New or second-hand, your baby's mattress should be kept clean at all times.

Chapter seven

Getting to know your baby

During the early days after delivery you may experience a strange mixture of emotions. One moment you are exhilarated and on top of the world, bursting with a sense of deep satisfaction and relief at having come through labour and delivered your baby; at other times you may feel confused and exhausted by the physical demands of feeding and caring for a new baby and the lack of time for yourself.

Your body seems strange and unfamiliar. During the last weeks of pregnancy you may have longed to be a 'normal' shape and size, rid of the excess weight and the twinges and discomforts of late pregnancy. However, in reality your body after delivery is far from 'normal'. Your abdomen seems empty and floppy, you are bleeding and sore around your vagina and perineum, and your breasts may feel hard, lumpy and uncomfortable as your milk supply becomes established.

You may also find that you miss the movements of your baby inside you and feel a sense of sadness that he is no longer carried safely within you. All that waiting and anticipation is over; a feeling of anti-climax is hardly surprising.

Do not expect too much of yourself during the first phase of motherhood. You and your baby are getting to know one another all over again. There are no set patterns or routines; try to take each day as it comes, without too many preconceived ideas of how things 'ought' to be.

One or two nights with very little sleep and a fretful baby do not mean that the next six weeks are going to be the same. Your baby is learning to recognise a welter of strange, physical sensations, e.g. hunger, tiredness, warmth, the feeling of clothes on his skin and the feeling of your arms and your partner's around him. Light, dark, noise have all been experienced from within the muffled, cocooned security of your body. Now he is being exposed to these stimuli without you to act as a shield. Gradually he will settle and you will be able to judge his needs.

Try to handle him gently and quietly. Feed him whenever he is hungry; do not leave him to cry. A calm, contented baby is one who has learnt that his needs will be met. Very quickly you will recognise whether he is hungry, uncomfortable, tired or just in need of your reassuring presence. Like you, he probably misses the intimate contact that existed between you before the birth.

If you had your baby in hospital, once

you get home the temptation is to try to run the house as you always have, fitting in housework, shopping and cooking around his sleeping times.

This is a big mistake. Accept offers of help and forget about housework for a while. It takes at least six weeks for breastfeeding to become established and during that time you should avoid all heavy chores like shopping. In the next few months you will build a workable routine; now you need to focus

Fathers can play an active role in looking after the new baby too. They can help with bottlefeeding expressed or formula milk, changing nappies and bathtime. This helps to give you some time to yourself if you are feeling tired and need a break from the routine of looking after your baby.

your energies on you and your baby. If you are not breastfeeding you still need to rest as much as you can. Enjoy this special time

Get to know your baby

alone with your baby – the chores can wait.

Most of this book has been addressed to mothers but fathers have a vital role to play. Try to take at least a week off work to be at home with your partner and your new son or daughter. Get involved with changing nappies and at bathtime. If your wife is not breastfeeding you too can feed the baby. You may feel at a disadvantage if your partner has 'learnt' how to do all these things in hospital but they are simple procedures and you will be amazed at how soon you feel confident in handling your child.

You can also help by taking charge at home. Limit the number of visitors and take responsibility for ushering them in and out of the house. Make sure your partner rests each day and do not be afraid to ask visitors to leave if she seems tired. Try to anticipate her needs. She may not like to ask you to take the initiative, but most women will feel deep gratitude towards partners who provide strong emotional and physical support.

You may already be used to sharing domestic chores but if you are not, now is the time to take over the shopping and cooking. Keep housework to a minimum; leave yourself time to enjoy these precious early days as a family and to lay firm foundation stones for your life together. In the UK, your health visitor will be able to offer you advice on all the practicalities of life at home with a new baby.

The role of the health visitor

Health visitors are all qualified nurses who have undergone further training in the care of people in the community. They are

Breastfeeding will give your baby the healthiest, best possible start in life as your milk contains the right balance of nutrients for growth, and helps protect your baby against infection and allergy. It may take some weeks to get established so don't give up.

interested in promoting good health and preventing ill-health. Health visitors are either attached to doctors' surgeries, or based in health centres. They work with all sections of the community but particularly parents with young children. You may meet your health visitor ante-natally; if not, she will visit you around the tenth day following delivery. She will continue to visit you or see you at the child health clinic where she will be able to advise on all aspects of child health.

Chapter eight

Getting back in shape

Many women expect their bodies to revert back to their pre-pregnancy shape soon after birth, and are dismayed when they find out that their stomachs are still flabby and it is more difficult then they anticipated to shift the extra weight they put on over the last nine months. Don't expect your figure to shrink miraculously back to normal immediately – it won't. Of course, you will look slimmer but your stomach muscles will be loose and you will need to exercise regularly to tone up your waist, abdomen, hips and thighs. However, don't be surprised if your body is never quite the same again. However hard you try to regain your original figure in the coming months, your breasts may sag a little and your stomach may never be quite so flat as it was before you became pregnant.

Breastfeeding will also help you to get back into shape and regain your figure. The fat stored by your body during pregnancy in

Important

Before you do the exercises shown in the following pages, check with your doctor or midwife that it is safe for you to do so. If you feel any pain or discomfort, stop immediately.

Exercising safely

Remember that your muscles and joints will be weaker than normal for a few weeks after the birth so do not attempt anything too strenuous for at least six weeks. Ask your doctor if you are unsure. As a general rule you should:
- Always move smoothly and slowly without any jerkiness.
- Only contract and tighten muscles for as long as feels comfortable.
- Do only the recommended exercises – not the ones you used to do at aerobic classes.
- Breathe deeply while exercising and relax between repetitions.

preparation for lactation will be used up very gradually in your daily milk production. Even though you cannot diet or cut down on your food at this time, if you eat a nutritious diet and avoid too many fatty, fried and sugary foods, then you will eventually lose weight.

Your midwife or doctor or the physiotherapist in the hospital where you give birth will be able to advise you on the best and safest postnatal exercises, and when

Getting back in shape

you should start these. If you have had a Caesarean section, there are special gentle exercises that you can do, particularly those that exercise the pelvic floor muscles. Ask your doctor for advice.

It is important not to exercise too strenuously in the early weeks after birth.

You can build up gradually and gently as your body heals and your strength and energy return. In hospital you will be shown some exercises to start you off. These will focus on your abdominal, waist and pelvic floor muscles.

Although looking after a young baby is a

Postnatal exercises: tummy tightener

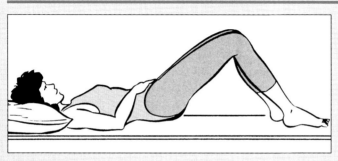

Lie on the bed or floor with a pillow under your head and shoulders. Bend your knees, inhale and lift your ribs. Exhale, lowering your ribs and pulling in your abdominal muscles towards your back. Relax, then repeat 5 times.

Postnatal exercises: bridging

Lie on your back with feet hip distance apart and knees bent. Squeeze and lift your pelvic floor muscles and raise your hips off the bed. Relax and lower your hips. Repeat 5 times.

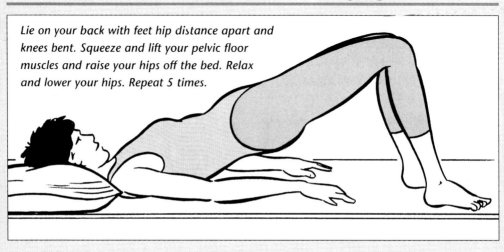

demanding and full-time job and leaves you little time for yourself in the early days, it is important to put aside at least 10 minutes a day for some gentle postnatal exercises.

Pelvic floor exercises

It is very important to start exercising your pelvic floor muscles and restore their tone after your baby is born. If you fail to do this, there is an increased risk of an inability to hold water or a prolapsed womb in later life. You can practise these exercises several times a day – sitting, standing or lying down.

There is no need to worry about your stitches. In fact, exercise will increase the blood flow to the area and promote speedier healing. Just squeeze and lift the muscles around the front passage as if you were trying to interrupt a stream of urine. Hold for a count of 3 and then relax. Practise the pelvic floor exercises that you learnt during pregnancy too(see page 34).

Postnatal posture

Posture is as important now as it was during pregnancy. Leaning over to breastfeed your baby and carrying him around can put additional strain on weakened back muscles. If you had a backache labour or an epidural, your back may still be sore and painful.

In pregnancy, the hormones softened and stretched the spinal and pelvic ligaments in preparation for childbirth, and it may take several weeks, or even months, for your back to return to normal. Finding a comfortable position for breastfeeding can help relieve

Postnatal exercises: roll overs

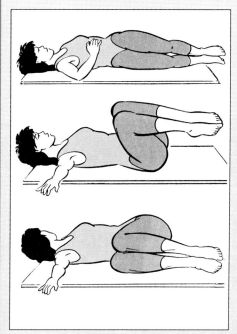

Lie on the floor or bed with your hands on your chest, and roll your legs with knees slightly bent over to the right. Stretch your arms out to the sides and roll up and over to the other side. Now roll your legs up and over to the right side but still facing to the left. Perform the movements smoothly without jerking. Repeat 5 times to each side. Some physiotherapists recommend that you do not attempt this exercise until the second week after birth.

Getting back in shape

any backache you may experience. Other tips include the following:

1 Bend your knees when lifting objects, and do not stoop or lift heavy objects for the first six weeks after birth.
2 Wear a baby sling that carries your baby centrally.
3 Use a pram or buggy with handles at waist level so you need not lean forwards to push it.
4 Do not slump in a chair; sit with a supporting cushion in the small of your back and your bottom pressed into the chair-back.
5 When you lift the baby out of his cot, lower the side and bend your knees to lift him up.
6 Try to bath your baby at waist level to avoid bending down.
7 Walk tall, tucking in your stomach and buttocks.
8 To relieve backache, do the angry cat exercise shown on page 41.

Postnatal exercises: knee lifts

1

1 Start on all-fours with your knees and hands in line with your hips and shoulders respectively. Breathe in and then breathe out slowly, raising your right leg up towards your chest. 2 Inhale and extend the right leg out behind you, keeping it slightly bent and your head and spine level. Repeat this exercise 5 times with each leg.

2

Postnatal exercises: leg sliding

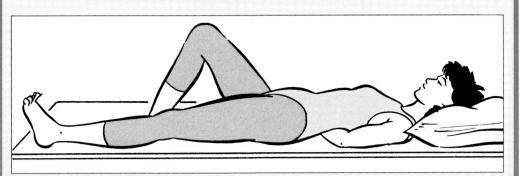

Lie down with your head and shoulders on a pillow. Bend one leg and straighten the other, flexing your outstretched foot. Slide your bent leg down as you pull the other one up into a bent knee position. Repeat 5 times with each leg.

Postnatal exercises: buttock lifts

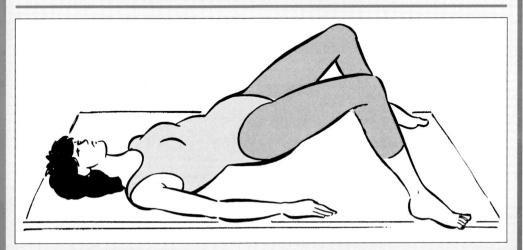

Lie on your back with your knees bent and feet flat on the floor. Slowly lift your hips and lower back off the floor until your body is in a straight line from knees to shoulders. Try to tighten the buttocks. Hold, then relax and repeat the exercise 5 times.

Getting back in shape

Postnatal exercises: curl downs

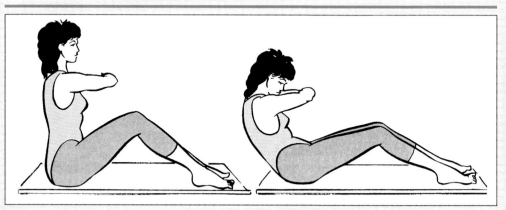

Note: only do the exercises shown on this page after consultation with your doctor. Sit with legs bent and arms folded. Lift your elbows to shoulder level. Breathe in, then exhale and lower your chin, leaning back until you feel your abdominal muscles tightening. Inhale and sit upright. Repeat the exercise 5 times.

Postnatal exercises: curl ups

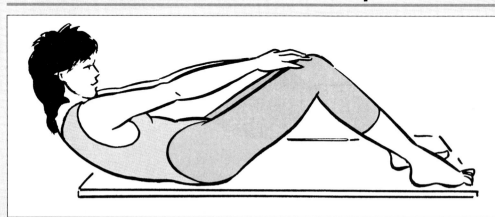

Lie on your back with knees bent and hands on thighs. Inhale, then breathe out and lift your head and shoulders slightly off the floor. Lower them gently to the floor, relax and then repeat 5 times. Stop immediately if you feel any pain.

Useful information

Here are some useful addresses and information if you wish to find out more about pregnancy and childbirth or to seek specialist help.

Preconceptual care

Foresight
28 The Paddock
Godalming
Surrey GU7 1XD
Tel: 0483 427839

Pregnancy and ante-natal care

Genetics Interest Group
Institute of Molecular
Medicine
John Radcliffe Hospital
Oxford OX3 9DU
Tel: 0865 744002

Harris Birthright Centre
Kings College Hospital
London
Tel: 071 326 3040

Health Visitors Association
50 Southwark Street
London SE1 1UN
Tel: 071 378 7255

LaLeche League
BM3424
London WC1N 3XX
Tel: 071 242 1278

Maternity Alliance
15 Britannia Street
London WC1X 9JP
Tel: 071 837 1265

National Childbirth Trust
Alexandra House
Oldham Terrace
Acton
London W3 6NH
Tel: 081 992 8637

Royal College of Midwives Trust
15 Mansfield Street
London W1M 0BE
Tel: 071 580 6523

United States

International Childbirth Education Association
PO Box 20048
Minneapolis
Minnesota 55420-0048
USA
Tel: 612 854 866

Maternity benefits in the UK

As a pregnant woman, you are entitled to certain rights and benefits. Your doctor or midwife should be able to give you some explanatory leaflets. If you have worked for the same employer for two years full-time or five years part-time before the twenty fifth week of pregnancy, you should be entitled to maternity leave from the twenty ninth week of pregnancy until twenty nine weeks after the birth. If you have changed jobs recently and are not eligible for maternity pay, you may be eligible for maternity allowance which is paid by your local social security office. Consult them for details.

Index

A

Acne, 8
Alcohol, 11
Alpha-feto-protein testing, 32
Amniocentesis, 32
Amniotic fluid, 39
Anaemia, 10, 17
Antenatal care, 15-17
Antenatal classes, 32-35
Antenatal exercises, 32-35
Apgar scores, 67

B

Baby clothes, 48-49
Baby equipment, 49-51
Backache, 41, 58
  in labour, 65
Bedding, 50
Birth choices, 21-22
Birth plan, 54
Bladder problems, 42
Blood supply, 30
Bottlefeeding, 55, 71
Braxton-Hicks contractions, 56
Breastfeeding, 10, 55, 67, 71, 72, 73
Breasts, 14
Breathing exercises, 53, 54
Breech birth, 63, 64
Bridging exercise, 45

C

Caesarean birth, 63, 64
Calcium, 9, 19
Carbohydrates, 8
Cerebral palsy, 68
Cervix, dilation of, 58
Childcare, 36
Colostrum, 55, 66
Constipation, 14, 42, 43
Contraceptive pill, 8
Contractions, 63, 65, 66
  Braxton-Hicks, 56
Cot death, 68-69

D

Dental care, 10, 20
Diabetes, 8
Diet, 17-19
Dilation of cervix, 58
Domino scheme, 21
Down's syndrome, 33, 68

Drugs, 8

E

Embryonic development, 25
Entonox, 64
Epidural, 63, 64
Episiotomy, 63, 65, 67
Exercise(s), 10, 20-21
  antenatal, 33, 34, 35
  bridging, 45
  pelvic floor, 34, 35
  postnatal, 73-78

F

Fertility, 8
Fertilization, 22-23
Fibre, 42
Folic acid, 9, 19

G

German measles, 11

H

Haemorrhoids, 43
Health visitors, 40, 68, 72
Heartburn, 43
High blood pressure, 8
Hormones, 14, 42
Horse riding, 20

I

Indigestion, 43
Iron, 9, 10, 42

K

Kick chart, 46

L

Labour, 59-63
  length of, 63
  positions for, 61-62
  signs of, 56
  types of, 59
Liver, 9

M

Morning sickness, 15

N

Nappies, 49
Nausea, 14, 15

O

Oedema, 44

P

Pain control, 64
Passive smoking, 11
Pelvic floor exercises, 34, 35, 75
Pethidine, 64, 65
Piles, 43
Placenta, 17, 28
  delivery of, 67
Postnatal exercises, 73-78
Posture, 30, 75
Preconceptual care, 7-12
Pre-eclampsia, 16
Protein, 8

R

Rectal separation, 35

S

Screening procedures, 16
Sexually transmitted diseases, 12
Sickle-cell anaemia, 17
Smoking, 11
Spina bifida, 33
Stretch marks, 46
Swelling, 44
Swimming, 10, 20

T

Tay Sachs disease, 17
Tests, 16, 17, 31-32
Thalassaemia, 17
Toxoplasmosis, 12, 17

U

Ultrasound scanning, 31
Uterus, 14, 29, 42

V

Varicose veins, 44
Vegetarian diets, 18
Vitamins, 9, 19

W

Waters breaking, 56
Weight gain, 17
Work, giving up, 36
Work hazards, 12

Y

Yoga, 20

Z

Zinc, 8, 19